Goal Setting & Team Management with OKR (Objectives and Key Results)

Skills for Effective Office Leadership, Smart Business Focus, & Growth. How to Manage Projects, People & Employees.

2nd Edition

By Thomas Pearson

Copyright

suitable for your situation. You should consult with a professional where appropriate. The accuracy and completeness of the information provided herein and the opinions stated herein are not guaranteed or warranted to produce any particular results, and the advice and strategies contained herein are not suitable for every individual. By providing information or links to other companies or websites, the publisher and the author do not guarantee, approve or endorse the information or products available at any linked websites or mentioned companies, or persons, nor does a link indicate any association with or endorsement by the publisher or author. It is offered or sold with the understanding that neither the publisher nor the author is engaged in rendering legal, accounting or other professional service. If legal advice or other expert assistance is required, the services of a competent professional should be sought. Neither the publisher nor the author shall be liable for any loss or loss of profit or any other commercial damages, including but not limited to special, incidental, consequential, or other damages.

Table of Contents

Ch. 1: Introduction

Inspiring a team of professionals to work together and achieve an ambitious goal, is not an easy undertaking. So how do you do it?

- How can you motivate your team to commit themselves to a complex task?
- How do you ensure that every member of your team is engaged in a productive pursuit—towards your company vision?
- How do you know which departments are working effectively, and which ones have stagnated?
- How do you inspire people to "stay the course" and pursue a higher purpose?

Here's the trick:

You need to move beyond mere "to-do lists" and accountability reports. It takes more than just a "quarterly employee review" to know if a worker is *really* producing for you. You need a more objective method to gauge productive output.

You need OKR!

So what is "OKR" you ask?

OKRs are an organizational framework, for setting company goals and tracking work progress. This book will teach you how to set them up in your own workplace. But, more importantly, this book will teach you how OKRs allow you to cultivate an insanely effective team (a "dream team"). One that is ready to climb any obstacle, and attack any ambitious goal you assign to them.

Read on, and you'll understand why so many Silicon Valley companies (like Twitter, LinkedIn, and Google) have whole-heartedly adopted the OKR management technique themselves. So, without further ado, let us begin our introduction to OKR.

A Brief History of OKRs

OKRs are not a completely new concept. In fact, they're a set of time-tested goal-tracking techniques for business management— that have been refurbished, to meet the needs of professionals, working in the 21st century.

Similar ideas go back to the titans of management (like Henry Ford), who believed that business management could be broken down into a chain of processes. He understood that employee-output could be measured objectively. And that daily production capacity could be predicted and tuned.

During the 1950s, management guru Peter Drucker devised his schema for corporate "management goals." Up until then, everyone focused on raw numbers alone. The introduction of his concept certainly improved the numbers, but it also helped achieve specific ancillary targets. Drucker called this technique

"Management by Objectives" (or MBOs). At present, most of the Fortune 500 companies employ at least some of these goal-setting techniques. Some companies tend to set annual goals, and others employ a biannual goal-setting process. But the ultimate objective is the same—to more adequately measure organization-wide performance and progress.

Andy Grove

In the 1960s, Andy Grove, the de-facto co-founder of Intel, came up with the concept we're most interested in: OKR (Objectives and Key Results). Grove didn't attempt to merely rewrite Drucker's concept of "Management by Objectives" (MBOs). But instead, he concentrated on pairing (what he called) "key results" to his own metrics for organizational goals (objectives). According to Andy Grove, these "key results" must be time-fixed milestones that help the workforce move in the proper direction—of attaining future ambitious goals.

Another change that Grove made to the old school MBO method, was in his certainty that Objectives and Key Results must be allowed to flow from the bottom to the top of an organization. It must start at the grassroots level (the employees) and harmoniously flow upwards to the bigwigs upstairs, and back down again—in a circuitous fashion. This introduced a sense of "employee empowerment" with the process. Because, until then, it was typical for companies to simply establish highfalutin targets, and then shove the responsibility down—through the organization's floors—to the lower employees. But Andy Grove's method gave his team leaders more freedom to work toward the vision of upper management, while not being constrained by it.

Another concept Grove introduced was (what he called), the "stretch goal." These are goals that are almost impossible to achieve fully. Andy Groves was fond of saying:

"70% is the new 100%."

Meaning that if only 70% of a goal was achieved, then this alone would be excellent—because the initial goal itself was so overtly ambitious, that even accomplishing a *mere fraction* of the goal was quite satisfactory.

This bold framing of goals (these "stretch goals") tends to have a positive psychological effect on employees—encouraging them to aim high, and think outside the box. (We'll be talking about "stretch goals" a lot in this book.)

John Doerr

During the latter part of the 1990s the OKR framework spread throughout Silicon Valley like wildfire. It all started with John Doerr, a partner in one of the country's most successful venture capital firms—Kleiner Perkins. Doerr was familiar with OKRs, because he had worked at Intel, under the leadership of Andy Grove. And he implemented them in Silicon Valley with great zeal.

Once the other companies in the valley started to notice Grove's success, they soon followed suit—by adopting similar OKR systems, and tweaking them to their needs.

Google

One of the best OKR success stories is none other than Google. The entire company, from the senior echelon of management to all the employees under them, set their OKRs quarterly, a practice that works well for the fast-paced world of Web 2.0 tech. At Google, every employee sets their OKRs digitally, and the information is made public throughout their company intranet. This allows for harmonious transparency of goal-setting. The OKRs at each level are accessible and visible to each and all. So if any given team is not in alignment, it will automatically stand out—making goals easier to grade and modify.

It is these attributes of "goal transparency" and "objectivity" that make OKR such a rich management method for the contemporary (technologically-enabled) workplace. And once you come to understand and appreciate their value, you'll find it easy to understand why so many tech companies have been quick to adopt them.

Ch. 2: What are OKRs?

Now that you know a bit about the history (and utility) of OKRs, you're probably still asking yourself: ***"What the hell are OKRs?"***

In one sentence:

OKRs are a framework for attaining organizational objectives, by employing a simple system for goal-setting, and progress tracking.

Remember, the OKR acronym stands for "Objectives and Key Results." So, there are two parts to an OKR:

- There are the "**Objectives**,"
- and there are the "**Key Results**."

Of course.

Let's talk about the Objectives first.

OKR Objectives

What is an OKR "objective"?

It's simply an "ambitious goal" for your company. Now, you must be careful to not choose a goal that is too ethereal, like:

- "I want to be rich."
- "I want my company to grow."
- "I want to make a lot of money."

We all want to make more money. But these goals are too vague to be OKR Objectives.

According to Andy Grove, OKR objectives should be: "qualitative, time-bound, actionable, and ambitious."

For example, suppose you ran an insurance company, and getting users to sign up at your website's application form, was how you garnered paying subscribers. (i.e. getting people to sign up to your website is how you make money.) Thus, decreasing the length and complexity of your website's signup process, would have obvious value to you.

So, instead of making a trite goal like: **"I want more money"** or **"I want more customers"** a better goal (what we call the "OKR objective") might be:

> "By next quarter, I want to reduce the amount of time it takes users to sign up to my website by half."

That's a nice objective.

For companies with detailed web forms, (like insurance companies, financing, or mortgage companies), this can be a fruitful goal, with obvious monetary benefit. And because of the complexity of such web forms, cutting the signup time down by half is quite ambitious.

Recall the quote from Andy Grove again: "70% is the new 100%." Thus, even if your team doesn't fully succeed in this objective, that's ok. Because achieving a fraction of this goal will boost your number of subscribers and (of course) make you more money.

So that covers the first letter in our OKR acronym. The "O" stands for "Objectives."

OKR Key Results

The "KR" stands for "Key Results."

So, what are Key Results?

Key Results describe the methods and the metrics by which we'll make our goal a reality. Typically, you should choose three or four Key Results per Objective.

Recall our OKR Objective again. It was:

"By next quarter, I want to reduce the amount of time it takes users to sign up to my website by half."

So let's brainstorm, and list three Key Results that would help us complete this objective.

- Key Result #1: Interview 100 customers and ask them to describe why they found our website too complicated to use.
- Key Result #2: Decrease the amount of time it takes our webpage to process the user's form input by 5 seconds.
- Key Result #3: Determine if there are any fields we can eliminate from our web form, to reduce the number of steps in our signup process.

So, notice that our three Key Results are the kinds of tasks you could see yourself working on, tracking, and delegating to your website team.

If your team accomplishes these tasks, then you'll be on your way to achieving your objective.

Key Results are not merely lines in a to-do list. Rather, as you glance at our three Key Results, you'll notice that each one is:

- quantifiable,
- objectively gradable,
- ambitious,
- and achievable.

Key results typically contain a numerical value, and they must be trackable over time. Thus, they can be based on many criteria, like growth, performance, engagement, or revenue. But of utmost importance, a Key Result is objectively gradable so its fulfillment is not open to interpretation.

Review Section

Let's briefly review this again, so you can get this concept down pat.

Again, OKR is a management framework. The acronym stands for "Objectives and Key Results."

What is an "Objective?"

An objective is a specific goal for your company. Our example was:

"By next quarter, I want to reduce the amount of time it takes users to sign up to my website by half."

Fulfilling this objective would be obviously fruitful for our example insurance company, and it provides our team with a clear destination to work towards.

Think of the OKR Objective as a destination, on your journey to success.

What is a "Key Result?"

A Key Result is a metric with a target to hit. Key Results help measure the progress we've made towards achieving our main OKR Objective.

Recall, in our example, Key Result #1 was:

"Interview 100 customers and ask them to describe why they found our website too complicated to use."

You can use your key results the same way you'd use milestones on a long journey. They are markers on the road, which let you know that you're progressing "on the right track"—toward your objective.

About the confusing names

Some readers find the terminology in OKR (Objectives and Key Results) confusing. They understand what an "Objective" is, of course. But the "Key Results" terminology is a little bit weird.

As John Doerr says:

"The Objective is what you want accomplished.

The Key Result is 'how I'm gonna get that done.'"

The reason the second part of the phrase "Key Results" is confusing, is because (in English) the word "result" is often used in a similar fashion to the word "goal." As in:

*"I worked in this mine for 10 years and, as a **result**, I got rich discovering diamonds."*

In this sentence, the result of the speaker's labor is similar to his work goal—his goal was to find diamonds and get rich. But, in OKR, the "Key Result" term is not referring to our future ultimate goal. Rather, the Key Results are referring to the little milestones we pass, (at key points) along the way toward achieving our main "Objective."

Personally, instead of the term "Key Results," I would have chosen a different name here. Perhaps the term "Key Milestone Metric" is better than the term "Key Result."

But, in any case, we are stuck with this name for now. We'll have to live with it. But, I just wanted to take a moment to bring this potential confusion to your attention. If the term "Key Results" confuses you, you're not alone.

Just remember, in OKR (Objectives and Key Results):

- The "Objective" is the future specific goal you want to achieve.
- And, the "Key Results" are the three or four distinct measurable tasks which help gauge your progress—and tell you if you're on course to achieving this Objective. Remember, each OKR Objective should have about 3 or 4 associated Key Results.

Another OKR Example

So, with that said, let's go through another OKR example.

Suppose our OKR Objective is to:

"Double our website traffic by next quarter."

This is a good OKR objective because it has a measurable metric (i.e. double our website traffic numbers), and an established timeframe (i.e. "by next quarter").

So, for this Objective, our Key Results might be:

- Key Result #1: Write and publish at least 10 new web articles per month.
- Key Result #2: Contact 20 website owners in my niche, and ask if I can interview them for my podcast.
- Key Result #3: Start an email list and attempt to sign up 25% of my existing customer base.

Notice that each of our three Key Results have an objectively established finish line.

- Write 10 articles.
- Contact 20 website owners.
- Sign up 25% of my customers.

So your Key Results can function as a type of to-do list. But they must have an associated quantifiable metric as well. So, when you're writing your Key Results, always ask yourself:

What values is this Key Result measuring?

If it takes you a while to answer this question, you might have chosen a bad Key Result. Because each Key Result should contain a blatantly obvious metric to pursue.

The value of OKRs

At the start of this chapter, we asked our hypothetical business-owner what his goals were. And he said, "I want to be rich."

Now that we have outlined the OKR process, I hope it's becoming clear to you how pithy his initial response was. And I hope you're beginning to see why adopting a *structured approach* to corporate goal-setting can be so fruitful.

This is the immense value that OKRs have to offer you. It shouldn't be a surprise that so many top Silicon Valley companies have adopted this technique. Starting with Intel, but later being picked up by Twitter, Zynga, LinkedIn, and Google.

OKRs reveal an obvious (but elusive) goal-setting technique, which you can employ at all levels of your company. And ensure that your employees are working in harmony, towards a shared corporate vision.

It's important that you comprehend the utility of OKRs, and that you understand how they're created, before continuing on with your OKR training. Don't be afraid to read this chapter again, if the concepts are still a bit fuzzy in your mind. In the least, you may want to practice writing down some good OKR Objectives for your own company. The rest of the OKR framework hinges upon this ability, so take it seriously.

As you become intimately familiar with OKR concepts, you might find yourself wondering how you ever ran your business without them!

Now, let's dive deeper, and learn more about OKRs.

Ch. 3: Are OKRs right for your company?

While everyone can benefit from adopting a structured (metric-based) goal-setting framework like OKR, the degree to which your company adopts OKR is up to you.

As mentioned previously, some Fortune 500 companies have implemented expensive, custom-designed software-based solutions for the tracking and monitoring of their employee OKRs. But other executives find that merely keeping a personal hand-written OKR logbook is sufficient to keep their company on track.

Not every company on the planet needs to force every single one of their employees to adopt OKRs. In this chapter, we'll help you figure out what level of adoption might work for your company.

Assess the Current Situation

Before you can implement OKRs, you will need to address a few critical questions. Some of these questions might seem trivial, but they're actually quite important—since they might reveal some underlying necessary facts about your company. The facts you obtain today, could play a major role—in helping you understand the process of setting goals with OKR.

The following questions should be addressed by the managerial and executive departments. Essentially, these questions need to be answered by all those who are responsible for the outcome of your corporate goals. And, it might help to carefully document your responses, because your corporate goals will (of course) change over time.

Here are some questions for the decision-makers:

- Question 1: Have we been setting any structured goals at all up until now? Do we have any pressing goals at the moment? (Note: A surprising number of companies don't even have one explicit goal, so it's ok if yours doesn't yet either.)
- Question 2: What was your original objective in setting up these goals?
- Question 3: Does the current status quo satisfy you?
- Question 4: Does any one of your existing management processes have obvious room for improvement?

Now, here are some questions for your employees, or the members of the team you manage:

- Question 1: Are you happy with the way goals are pursued now? Do you think the company needs a new framework for goal-setting?
- Question 2: How frequently do you update your current goals?
- Question 3: Does your manager share any feedback with you about your goal progress?

- Question 4: Do you think that the way we measure goals now is an objective measure of success or failure?
- Question 5: Is there a real connection between the daily tasks you perform, and the goals you set?
- Question 6: Do you think that you (and your team) have a fair say in choosing goals?
- Question 7: Do you feel that your goals inspire you, and motivate you to do better?
- Question 8: If you had an opportunity to change or improve the process of goal-setting, what are some things that you would suggest?

You may want to allow your employees to submit their answers anonymously. It makes the feedback less biased, and keeps everyone honest and objective. Of course, you can use free survey tools like Google Forms—to gather the responses digitally, and anonymously.

Also, be sure to thoroughly analyze your employee's feedback, and acknowledge his good ideas. And save your responses for future reference. When you look back on these responses in the future, you might be surprised how far you've come, and how things have changed in your company.

OKR Compatibility

As mentioned previously, OKRs are regularly used by tech titans like Google, LinkedIn, and Spotify. There's a reason why OKRs work so well for these organizations. All these companies have corporate values that resonate with OKR philosophy. Most importantly, they believe in transparency among the workforce, and in fostering a belief in a noble corporate vision.

Let's list a few key characteristics (critical company values and behaviors) that an organization should have, if it hopes to achieve successful OKR adoption.

#1. Transparency

Many companies take the conventional route of information-sharing, and operate on a "need to know" or "according to pay grade" basis. The OKR framework doesn't necessarily imply that an organization must share everything with all employees. But, they should strive to share as much as possible—for the given objective. Transparency fosters an environment of trust, and will inspire the employees along, in the right direction.

#2. A clear and ambitious goal

A clear purpose or vision is important in goal-setting. In large companies, it can sometimes seem that tasks are distributed from the "nameless gods on high" (corporate stiffs without a face). And when employees cannot intuit why their "chore of the day" would have any value, they are less motivated to do it.

In OKR, we try to keep the process of goal-setting ambitious. The companies that successfully use OKRs believe that it is important to challenge their employees with an inspiring and meaningful goal.

#3. High employee engagement

Almost any company that adopts OKRs will show an increase in employee engagement. But if your workplace already has high employee engagement, all the better. Such environments are most conducive to the adoption of OKRs.

Are OKRs compatible with Agile frameworks?

It seems like everything is *"agile"* these days.

The term "agile" pops up in many different corporate domains—particularly in various sectors of the tech industry. For example, there is agile employee engagement, agile software development, agile project management, etc.

Broadly speaking, an "agile" framework simply refers to a division of tasks into short segments of work, followed by frequent reassessment, and adaptation of plans. An agile methodology encourages employees to quickly assess the work they've accomplished, and make rapid course-corrections as needed.

So, what makes OKRs congruous with an "agile framework" for goal-setting?

Several things:

- OKRs welcome change, and encourage managers to discard goals that are not working.

- OKRs often use a system of regular check-ins and weekly updates, which help the team stay on track to finish goals.
- OKRs encourage communication and collaboration between corporate tiers. Management goals are reflected and complemented by the employees at the lower levels.
- And, OKRs encourage face-to-face communication during regular assessment meetings.

If you have an existing process of agile management, then OKRs should fit seamlessly into your existing schema of operations. OKRs tend to nicely compliment the spirit of agility, for both your short-term and long-term goals.

The Four Biggest Benefits of OKR

Do you have a destination in mind when you go on a leisurely hike with your family? Maybe not. And that's ok, for recreational outings.

But, when it comes to work, doddering around (without reason or purpose) is just bad business. Without a clear vision for your company, you'll end up wasting your time, as well as the time of your employees.

This should be obvious. Yet, as you get used to implementing OKRs in your own company, you might be surprised by the number of companies who wander around aimlessly, without any objectives at all.

OKRs can be a lifesaver for such companies. When you setup OKRs for your employees, you'll be giving them the gift of an established destination to head towards. This not only enhances productivity, but also reduces wasted time, effort, and capital.

Specifically, here are four major benefits of OKR. When implemented correctly, this is what you can expect to see in your own organization:

- Increased Focus
- Workforce Harmony
- Rapid Innovation
- and Employee Engagement

Let's explore each of these now.

#1. Increased Focus

What is it that you should (or should not) be doing as an organization?

What is it that your *employees* should (or should not) be doing?

It is obvious that "focus" improves when the organization has definitive goals to work towards. OKRs improve your ability to concentrate on specific objective tasks, and prioritize these tasks into a hierarchy of importance.

An organization, without any concrete objectives, will often falter. But when all the teams in an organization, and each individual employee, know what their clearly defined roles are, then productivity will (almost certainly) rise.

#2. Workforce Harmony

When each team and employee in your organization has followed the steps in the previous chapters, and is pursuing OKRs together, then, something magical happens. Suddenly there is harmony in your workforce—that resonates down from the lowest employee, to the top managers.

So long as the individual employee OKR goals are congruous with the organizational OKR goals (that define your corporate vision), then each and every employee can relax, and rest assured that their labor is not in vain, and is indeed in pursuit of the common good.

As Dick Costolo, the former CEO of Twitter, said in an interview:

"The thing that I saw at Google that I definitely have applied at Twitter are OKRs—Objectives and Key Results. Those are a great way to help everyone in the company understand what's important, and how you're going to measure what's important. It's essentially a great way to communicate strategy and how you're going to measure strategy. And that's how we try to use them. As you grow a company, the single hardest thing to scale is communication. It's remarkably difficult. OKRs are a great way to make sure everyone understands how you're going to measure success and strategy."

#3. Rapid Innovation

Recall again the famous quote from Andy Grove:

"70% is the new 100%."

With OKRs, we don't just establish goals, we establish "stretch goals." As described in the previous chapters, "stretch goals" are goals that are so ambitious, that, even if your employees only succeed in meeting 70% of the goal, then, this amount alone is actually quite fruitful. (Because the original goal was so ambitious.)

By employing "stretch goals," we signal an important message to the employees, and we allow the management to request a high threshold of success. This has the effect of continually encouraging employees to push themselves each and every day.

#4. Employee Engagement

Yet another benefit of OKR is increased "employee engagement."

Everyone likes to be acknowledged, particularly for labor that has an obvious purpose. When you give your employees "busy work," or when they fail to see the result of their efforts, then it's easy for employees to feel like their inputs are inconsequential. And this breeds negative emotions.

OKRs help to solve this issue. When the organizational objectives are harmonious, and publicly visible to every team and individual in the organization, then your workers can clearly comprehend how the work they do is positively contributing to the company. When it's apparent that, every inch of progress made, can add to the corporate journey, then this keeps everyone engaged at work.

OKRs won't solve all your problems

There is no doubt that the glamor of all the shiny Silicon Valley tech companies, successfully using OKRs, can be alluring. But don't make the mistake of believing that OKRs are the answer to all your corporate problems.

Again, the OKRs will not do you any good, if the underlying organizational values are ignored, or are incompatible. OKRs are not a "silver bullet," and will not eliminate all the problems that your business faces. Instead, OKRs will help you understand the existing problems, and help you come up with a plan to fix them.

Ch. 4: Implementing OKRs

In this chapter, we'll go over some fundamental OKR techniques, which you can employ once you've decided to implement OKRs in your workplace.

Now remember, you don't have to go overboard with this. When you're first starting out with OKRs, don't be tempted to hold 10-hour company-wide training programs, or invest in expensive OKR software. It's ok to start small. A pencil and paper will work just fine.

Instead, focus on the OKR goal-setting process we've outlined in the previous chapters. You don't need to be as big and ruthless as Google, to get value out of OKRs.

- Even if you only manage a small business (with only one or two employees), OKRs still work.
- Even if you only implement a couple OKRs in a non-essential department (just for testing purposes), that's ok. OKRs still work.
- Indeed, even if you use these OKR techniques for the fulfillment of your own personal life goals, that's ok too. OKRs still work.

Remember, at its core, OKR is just a goal-setting and goal-tracking technique. So if you've ever set any sort of goal in your life, you can probably benefit from OKRs.

Review Time

Let's review again briefly:

OKR stands for "Objectives and Key Results." There are two parts to an OKR:

- There's the "Objective,"
- and there are the (three or four) associated "Key Results."

In the previous chapters, we chose an insurance company as our sample business. And our OKR Objective was:

"By next quarter, I want to reduce the amount of time it takes users to sign up to my website by half."

That's a nice OKR Objective.

And then we chose three Key Results for this Objective. Let's list them again:

- Key Result #1: Interview 100 customers and ask them to describe why they found our website to be too complicated to use.
- Key Result #2: Decrease the amount of time it takes our webpage to process the user's form input by 3 seconds.
- Key Result #3: Determine if there are any fields we can eliminate from our web form, to reduce the number of steps in our signup process.

Notice that our Key Results are reminiscent of the kinds of tasks you'd give to a web development team in your company. They differ from a standard to-do list however, because they have objectively defined metrics, and they are attached to a time-bound objective.

So now that we have an Objective, and we have given our team three Key Results to work on, how much time will they need to accomplish them? Well the answer to that question varies of course. It depends on the sophistication of your team and the complexity of the goal.

But, the amount of time you give your employees to work on the problem, is called the "OKR Cadence" (which we'll talk about now).

Setting the OKR Cadence

The OKR "cadence" refers to the pace (or the "duration of time") that you'll give your team to work on the OKR. When the cadence is complete (when their time is up), this is when you assess your team's progress, and grade their Key Results.

Often, OKRs are reviewed on a quarterly basis (every three months). That's because, for many teams, the duration of one quarter is a sufficient amount of time needed to make headway toward completing an ambitious OKR Objective. But there is no "set-in-stone" rule about how much time you should give your team. The answer to that question depends on factors that only you are in a position to know.

But be warned:

- If the amount of time you give your team to accomplish the OKR is too **short**, then the task will seem impossible to them.
- If the amount of time you give your team to accomplish the OKR is too **long**, then there will be no urgency in its completion, and your team may be lackadaisical about it.

The trick is to choose a time-frame (an "OKR Cadence") that is short enough to encourage brisk action, but long enough to give your team time to focus and work.

- OKRs for smaller teams tend to do better with a shorter cadence. Perhaps about one to three months.
- While OKRs that are designed for the organizational level of a large company, may do better with a longer cadence. Perhaps half a year.

Here are some OKR Cadence Questions

When you're trying to decide how much time to give your team to work on their OKRs, ask yourself these questions:

Question 1: What stage of business am I at?
If you're running a new startup, and you don't even know if you'll exist in a month, then it's best to keep your OKR Cadence short. However, if you're a titan of industry, with your mind set on corporate takeovers, then adopting a long-term outlook is probably better.

Question 2: What skill level does my employee have?
If you're creating some OKRs for an employee that has been with your company for many years, then perhaps he can take on longer (more difficult and complicated) tasks. But if you just hired your

employee last week (and you're not sure if you're going to keep him), then shorter OKRs are best—e.g. use assignments that will only take a few days to complete.

Question 3: What is your industry like?

If you're in an industry that is susceptible to forces beyond your control, like bad weather, natural disasters, or airline worker strikes, then choosing short OKRs may be best. So you can have the flexibility to deal with chaotically changing market forces as they come. On the other hand, if your industry is historically predictable, then devising longer goals makes more sense.

In any case, the duration you choose for your OKR Cadence is up to you. And one organization need not use the same Cadence for every OKR.

How to Grade OKRs

When the duration of the OKR cadence is up, then it's time to grade your OKRs.

Recall, our OKR Objective from our example business:

"By next quarter, I want to reduce the amount of time it takes users to sign up to my website by half."

So, now that the duration of our OKR cadence is complete, we need to assign an "OKR Grade."

The most common way to grade OKRs, is to grade the Key Results on a scale of 0-10, and then to simply derive a grade for the "Objectives" according to the average grade of its corresponding Key Results.

Let's list our Key Results one last time here:

- Key Result #1: Interview 100 customers and ask them to describe why they found our website to be too complicated to use.
- Key Result #2: Decrease the amount of time it takes our webpage to process the user's form input by 3 seconds.
- Key Result #3: Determine if there are any fields we can eliminate from our web form, to reduce the number of steps in our signup process.

Grading OKRs is a practice intended to help you engage in objective self-assessment and refinement of our goals and techniques.

So how did our team do on our three Key Results?

- Did we manage to contact 100 customers?
- Is our web form working faster?
- Did we reduce the number of fields that the user has to fill out?

This is the point where we'd assign a grade to each Key Result. (A number from zero to ten.)

If the Key Result was accomplished completely, then give it a 10. If not, then give it a lesser score—depending on how close your employees got to successful completion.

Here are a couple of other things to keep in mind when grading OKRs:

Numerical grades do not always reflect the metrics at play in the OKR. Recall that, with OKRs we seek to pick lofty (hard to reach) objectives. We choose objectives, not because they are easy, but because they are hard.

Recall the famous Andy Grove quote again: *"70% is the new 100%."*

So if your team succeeded in fulfilling only 70% of their OKR objective, this doesn't mean you should give them a grade of "7." On the contrary, your team's original objective might have been extremely ambitious.

Say, their OKR Objective was to sign up a million new users to your software company. If your team succeeded in signing up only half that amount (500,000 users), then, that is still a very impressive performance! And this OKR probably deserves a grade of 10.

The opposite of this can be true as well. For example, if your team was able to complete 95% of their OKR objective, but the objective was not very impressive to begin with, (or the completion of the objective was due to ancillary inputs— unrelated to the team's Key Results), then this OKR would deserve a low grade.

Once you've assigned a grade to each OKR, sit back and ponder them as a whole. The grades of all previous OKRs should assist you in the development of new goals (of new OKRs)—for the next work cycle. And they should help you to evaluate the individual efforts of each team.

On a side note, the manager should be warned against using OKR grades as a foundation for "employee compensation." In other words, if you decide to start paying your employees based on how many OKR Objectives they've completed, then this might simply encourage them to choose less ambitious OKR Objectives. And you *really* don't want that!

It's ok to let your OKR review augment your analysis for the size of an employee's paycheck. But don't let OKRs influence your decision too much.

Understanding OKR Levels

There are three different types of OKRs—at the level of the:

- Organization,
- the Team,
- and the Individual Employee

Just as the task that you'd assign to an individual employee, is not the same as the task you'd designate as an organization-wide goal, the OKRs you assign to an employee, also vary from the OKRs you'd assign to your "top-level management."

Let's discuss these levels now.

Level 1: Organizational Level OKRs

OKRs are forward-looking tools, for goal setting. So, not only do we want to encourage immediate day-to-day performance, but we also want to pave the way for future success.

In a company, if you exclusively concentrate on a narrow outlook of immediate goals, then, you'll lose the big picture. So, it's important to ensure that your top-level OKRs are established in such a manner that they, not only help you achieve the targets in the current work cycle, but also give you a footing for the next cycle too.

Important Tips

So here are a few tips for creating Organizational Level OKRs:

1. The OKRs should be derived from (or congruous with) your company's vision statement. If your corporate vision is about creating the best superconductors in the world, and your OKR is about developing a new TV show, then there is probably something "out of whack" here.
2. The OKRs should be transparent, (or as transparent as possible), to all other employees.
3. The OKRs should be applicable (and actionable) by the top-level management team.
4. It's best to work on these "company-level OKRs" first, before working on the team and employee level OKRs. This helps to solidify your corporate vision—from the top to the bottom.

Level 2: Team Level OKRs

Now we move to the second level of OKRs—the "team level."

The composition of a team always varies of course—from one organization to another.

Some organizations have cross-functional teams, while others assemble only temporary teams—that might come together for just one project. So, you must design your Team Level OKRs according to the methodology in play at your own workplace.

Contrary to the traditional process of goal-setting—wherein the team manager is always responsible for deciding the team's goals, the OKR framework involves *all team members*, and it's a collaborative process. The alignment of your team OKR, and the employee OKR is possible, only when all members are actively participating in deciding the goals together.

Here are some tips to use when developing your "Team-level OKRs."

1. One team leader (perhaps your team manager), should take responsibility for monitoring the OKRs, and making sure that OKR metrics are being tracked.
2. The team-level OKRs should complement the OKRs of the company vision as a whole.
3. All the OKRs must be created collaboratively (with the whole team involved), and must not be decided upon by only one member.

Level 3: Individual Employee Level OKRs

And finally for the third and final level, the "Employee Level OKRs." There are various schools of thought when it comes to setting up OKRs for individual employees. There are no hard and fast rules here. And you have to tailor the OKR framework to your own employee management style, while considering your work culture and team dynamics.

It's easy to confuse the individual employee OKRs, with the Team OKRs. In fact, some companies find that it's better to not have *any* OKRs at the employee level at all. This is because, these days, individual employees (especially in tech startups) function in close-knit groups. These teams might have less than a half-dozen people, and the groups are so intimate, that multiple employees can be perceived as singular individual "working units."

In such cases, you may consider just ignoring this third level of individual employee OKRs, and stick to using only two OKR levels. Also, if you are just getting started with OKRs, be sure to set them up for the organizational and team levels first. And, only then, consider how your individual employees feel about adding this additional third "employee level OKR."

Remember, you don't have to change the world in one day. You can refine this process over time, and consider introducing individual employee OKRs gradually—after you feel more confident about the adoption of the OKR framework in general.

Setting up OKRs with Your Team

OKRs are the "hot new management style on the block." But, before diving in with OKRs, it's best to identify the parts that are already working well, in your current goal-setting system. (Assuming you have one.)

In other words, the OKR framework does not necessarily have to replace every existing system—currently in use at your company. So if you have a schema that's working for you, don't make the mistake of throwing the baby out with the bathwater. Instead, it's ok to morph the OKR schema to suit the needs of your existing one.

There is always room for improvement and adaptation with OKRs. There is no "one size fits all" OKR solution for everyone. And, even if your OKR framework is working flawlessly one year, this doesn't mean that you shouldn't change it in the years to come—as the market (and your company) evolves.

Indeed, it is wise to encourage your OKR managers to be mindful of what's working (and what's not), and to be open to change. There is no "right or wrong" way to do this, and you must never forget the agile principle of management:

"People always come before processes."

Let your employees in on the Process of OKR Improvement

As with learning any new system, the first time you use the OKR system can be stressful for a company. Inevitably, various issues will arise, that you just aren't prepared for. So it's best to not keep anyone in the dark. Conduct team-level OKR reviews, and company-level OKR reviews, a few times per year.

Additionally, it's important to foster an environment of open sharing—where employees are free to express their honest opinions, without worrying about any negative consequences.

Use anonymous surveys to gauge OKR effectiveness if you think people are shy about speaking up.

Here are a few questions you might ask:

- On a scale of one to ten, do you think the OKRs were effective last quarter? Why or why not?
- What would have made the OKRs useful last quarter? What could we have added, to make them more effective?
- Is there any other idea or metric that we should be focusing on? One that we didn't focus on last quarter?

Additionally, try to include open-ended questions in your survey. And remember, it's not enough just to gather questionnaires at the end of the quarter, and toss them in the trashcan (like most corporations do).

Instead be prepared to act upon the data, and modify your OKRs based on the feedback. Hold meetings, and try to understand the concerns of your employees.

Are your employees actually using their OKRs?

You should have some way to track OKR adoption.

Typically, you should be maintaining a log of progress updates from your team. And they should be made aware of when these updates are expected—throughout the quarter. Encourage your team members to get in the habit of frequently updating their OKRs.

- How many customers did they call this week?

- Were they able to successfully complete any Key Results this week?

Your employees should have this sort of information available for you. Again, you do not need to invest in expensive software, or create a complex OKR digital reporting system. Pencil and paper will do fine. The point of these mini reports is merely to make sure that each member is progressing along.

Inevitably, you'll notice that certain people aren't updating their OKR stats as frequently as you had hoped. Pushing a new workflow on an employee (set in his ways) can be grueling. But don't shove OKRs down his throat on day one.

Instead, work to get him (and the rest of your team) to appreciate the rich value that OKRs can eventually bring forth. Be patient. The implementation of OKRs will take time. But when reasonable employees see that your new system actually has value, they will come to adopt it.

Employee Onboarding

When you're ready to adopt OKRs whole-heartedly, then be prepared to make some changes to the way work usually gets done in your office. It's typically best to avoid the element of surprise, and rollout OKRs gradually, as you implement the schema across various levels of your business.

Introduce them in phases, by conducting OKR workshops or training sessions—at least two to three weeks prior to insisting on OKR adoption. Such sessions can be conducted by OKR expert corporate trainers, of course. But often, it's best if an existing member of your team becomes familiar with OKRs first, and then helps to train his coworkers. Remember, what's most important is that your employees come to understand and appreciate the value of creating their goals according to the OKR framework we laid out at the beginning of this book.

Typically, companies will select at least one individual to be the "OKR champion." Such an individual will be responsible for ensuring that OKRs are being implemented properly by the team, and that his coworkers understand how to create OKR Objectives and pursue (and track), their Key Results. The main goal is to ensure that all those involved in the business are gradually exposed to what OKRs are, how they work, and how they are being tweaked to meet the specific needs of the organization.

Early on in this process, it is wise to conceive of some ideal set of expectations that you wish to fulfill by using OKRs. You must clearly define what success and failure look like—for various time frames. You can use the results that you procured from the anonymous surveys in the previous section, to help with this goal. And it's best if you create some documentation—defining success and failure in unambiguous terms.

Ch. 5: How to Set Goals

As you know, the first letter in our OKR acronym is the "O" for "Objectives." So, let's talk a little about the importance of choosing ambitious and inspirational objectives now.

In a more perfect world, I wouldn't have to bring up the necessity of using structured goals. Every manager already understands the value of goal-setting right?

Wrong.

You might be surprised at the number of managers I've met (in companies big and small) who operate without any definitive goals at all. Or, more commonly, they do set goals (of a sort), but the goals have no objective metric—by which anyone would know how far along the company is, in the goal's completion.

So let's talk about the importance of applying a structured goal-setting paradigm like OKR. Such goals are the only way to really *objectively* measure success. But not just success. Goals also act as the *barometer* by which you know you're moving in the right direction.

In this chapter, we'll talk about the benefits to be had, by utilizing "structured goal-setting" in your organization.

Why Goals Matter

Goals are Your Compass

First, writing out a goal for yourself or your company, establishes a psychological compass, that (ideally) points us toward the fulfillment of our corporate vision. Even if you're working hard, you (or your company) might still suffer from a "lack of direction." It's quite possible (and indeed common) to encounter large corporations full of "busy idiots"—people who look busy but aren't really doing anything. If you don't know where you're headed, then, even if you do manage to stumble upon the right path, you may not even know you're on it?

Goals Get Results

The most successful people in this world (from Michael Phelps to Bill Gates), regardless of their profession, set daily, weekly, and yearly goals for themselves. Whenever you set a goal, you give your team a vision to work towards. It helps to continually ensure that you are pushing yourself to attain better and better results. Opportunities will come your way, but you need to be ready to grab them.

Goals encourage you to take more action than you otherwise would. Whenever your brain is engaged in the activity of "goal-setting" your mind is set in a forward-thinking mode. And, as you progress through your workday, your subconscious will be quietly working to align your little daily actions with your ultimate objectives.

Goals Help Your Team Focus

A sense of purpose improves one's ability to focus. Setting goals for a team helps to align their thoughts and concentration to the task at hand. Even if the current obstacle is intimidating, your team will need to focus, and pull together to begin their climb. And, because OKR Objectives are explicitly defined, they help your team to "stay the course," and prevent them from making the mistake of wandering around, wasting time on some other insignificant (but easier) task.

Goals Create Accountability

Goals make people accountable. Team-level goals in particular can be infinitely effective, because they leverage our basal need for social acceptance. We have an innate human drive to "not let the team down." And publicly proclaiming our goals (as we do when we set Objectives with OKR), has the benefit of inciting team motivation and healthy social pressure.

Goals encourage you to be your best

Perhaps because of the transparent nature of OKR goal-setting, such public declarations help you to unlock the full potential of your team.

Without any challenging goals at all, they will be obliged to stick to whatever comfortable routine they've been stuck in for years gone by. Comfort is one of the most significant hurdles to success. Neither you, nor your team, can ever achieve success if you aren't willing to step out of this comfort zone. This is why the concept of the OKR "Stretch Goal" is so important. Because they cause us to break free—from these self-imposed limitations and encourage us to do better.

Conventional Goal-Setting

So, how do we set goals? The conventional recipe goes something like this:

Step 1

First, you identify a problem area that needs your attention. What do you want to change, about your workplace (or your life), right now? It can be your morning routine, eating habits, or the way you manage your employees.

Step 2

Then you map out the first couple action steps that you'll need to take, to get the ball rolling. Your first few steps don't have to be perfect. Far from it! As we've tried to stress in the previous section, it's more important that you just start.

Step 3

Prepare yourself for all likely outcomes. We can never know 100% of the possible outcomes of course. But, the more contingencies you plan for, the less surprised you'll be, when they actually occur.

You can gauge whether you are prepared or not, by asking yourself a few simple questions.

- Have you thought about which obstacles you will encounter?
- Can you think of ways to avoid these obstacles, if they arise?
- Do you have all the resources you need, to get the job done?

When you can answer these questions in a (somewhat) satisfying fashion, then you are ready to take your first step, toward the accomplishment of your goal.

Problems with Conventional Goal-Setting

The above-described steps are ok. But, they're not enough. Conventional organizational goal-setting typically entails assigning vague goals to employees—based on their job titles. In this manner, "goals" are often confused with the employee's "job description." And this is a fallacy we want to avoid. Many companies assign a goal to an employee on his first day of work. And then, his goal remains unchanged—sometimes for decades. This "set it and forget it" strategy leads to stagnation, and results in an apathetic workforce.

Sometimes, companies will fail to define what exactly "success and failure" would mean to a goal. You may come across extremely vague company goals like:

- "Maintain the quality control of deliverables."
- "Be responsible for upholding the values of the company."

When you actually analyze goals like this, you'll quickly realize that they don't really mean anything. These goals can't be measured. They are "open to interpretation" and too ethereal to be of much use. The value of having a "metric-based goal-setting plan" (like OKR) is an obvious improvement.

When it comes to reviewing company goals (i.e. seeing if your employees are accomplishing anything at all), most companies we've encountered either only conduct annual reviews, or none at all. Goals are sometimes used as a "crude yardstick"—for backward-looking performance reviews.

Please be warned that such observations do not necessarily mean that conventional goals do not work in some fashion. Indeed, having *some* sort of goal is better than no goal at all. And for occupations requiring low-skilled labor (with little cognitive demand), perhaps having complex goals and metrics is not always fruitful.

But, for businesses that require a modicum of cognitive effort, then conventional processes are typically in need of a makeover. This is why we are so enthusiastic about the OKR framework.

Goal-Setting with S.M.A.R.T.

Sometimes, new managers or new business owners have trouble getting in the "goal-setting frame of mind." It could be that, you're too used to thinking of corporate goals as a sort of ethereal, far off destination. Perhaps your goals only exist as a hazy one-liner from your job description, and you find yourself mindlessly trudging toward its fulfillment (each Monday morning), but you're never quite sure how much ground you've managed to gain (if any).

Before you start thinking too critically about any given OKR Objective, it can be helpful to brainstorm about goals first. So, to help jump-start the goal-setting gears in your head, let's talk about the "**SMART goal-setting Criteria**."

What is SMART?

SMART is an acronym that stands for:

- **S**pecific,
- **M**easurable,
- **A**ttainable,
- **R**ealistic,
- **T**ime-bound.

It's a "goal-setting criteria," developed by George Doran in 1981, and published in Management Review magazine—featured as an article entitled: *"There's a S.M.A.R.T. way to write management's goals and objectives."* Doran's "SMART system" breaks down the goal-setting chore, into five easy-to-remember steps. It's hard to write a management book without at least mentioning SMART. And there may be some utility in thinking about company goals via a SMART framework, before setting down more rigid goals via OKR.

Let's walk through the SMART steps now.

SMART Step 1: S if for "Specific"

You must have a specific goal in mind. Setting a vague goal like, "I want to be rich" is not a SMART goal. It's not specific enough. The word "rich" means different things to different people. Instead, a SMART goal would look something like this:

"I want to retire at age 55, with 10 million dollars in the bank."

This goal is better, because it contains metrics we can use to gauge whether or not we're on the right track.

SMART Step 2: M is for "Measurable"

Once you have your stated goal in mind, you must determine the objective metrics by which you will be measuring your progress—towards this goal's completion.

In our example above, the speaker wanted to be rich. And, 10 million dollars is his measure of *"rich."* So he'll know he is "rich," when he has 10 million dollars in the bank.

The point is, there is value in having a precise metric for delineating the completion of your goal. It helps to put the scope of your daily progress into perspective.

Anything that cannot be measured becomes difficult to manage?

SMART Step 3: A is for "Attainable"

You are setting yourself up for failure if there is no possible way you can ever attain your goal. If your goal is unattainable and unachievable, then your initial process of goal-setting was in vain.

Now remember, it's good to dream big. And achieving even a fraction of our goal of "earning 10 million dollars," may still be satisfactory. So aim high, but don't let yourself get discouraged by choosing targets that will never be reached.

SMART Step 4: R is for "Realistic"

The goal that you're setting must be realistic, given your current (or possible) available resources. If you want to start a new car company, and you have no background in engineering, and only $10 dollars in your pocket, then the goal of "starting a car company" is not a realistic goal.

Instead, your goal must be such that you can achieve it, following the execution of a careful plan of action, and lots of hard work, using resources at your disposal.

SMART Step 5: T is for "Time-bound"

You must always establish a deadline for achieving your goal. If you don't have a timeline in mind, then it is likely that your goal will never get done. Parkinson's Law states that:

"Work expands so as to fill the time available for its completion."

Meaning that, if you give yourself 10 hours to write your book report, then you'll do it in 10 hours. If you give yourself 10 weeks, then you'll do it in 10 weeks.

There will always be more work to do, on any given project. And, there will always be an excuse to not work on a project that day. This is a natural regression that you must learn to spot and avoid.

For instance, if your goal is to lose 30 pounds, then it will not make any sense unless you have a deadline. So re-phrase your goal statement as:

"I want to lose 30 pounds in three months."

Using SMART for OKR Inspiration

Remember that the SMART goal-setting criteria doesn't have to be rigid. It is more of a "recommended checklist" than a "plan of action."

For our purposes here, you can think of the SMART criteria as a "sketchpad"—where you briskly write out your goal-setting thoughts, and gather some perspective about what you'd like to see your team accomplish this year. Then, after you're comfortable with quickly creating metric-based and time-bound goals, apply these techniques each time you scribe a more structured "OKR Objective" for your team.

Ch. 6: When OKRs Fail

Failure is common.

Errors and mistakes are bound to happen. The vast majority of projects that have *ever* been attempted by a human, have failed. Even Google, the company that employs the smartest workforce on the planet, supports projects that fail constantly. The vast majority of Google products have either failed to complete, or failed to catch on—and had a short-lived lifecycle. The way your company deals with failure, is much more important than the failure itself. Be wary of punishing employee failure. This may scare the individual into being too risk-averse. And they may never strive to do innovative work for you ever again.

Recall the famous Thomas Edison quote:

"I have not failed. I've just found 10,000 ways that won't work."

Eventually, one of your teams will fail to meet their OKRs. At times, giving up might seem like the only option. And indeed, this is sometimes the best option. When your team experiences a crippling setback, now is the time to pull together and find out what went wrong. Seek out alternative sources of motivation, and don't get stuck in your ways if something is not working.

As the OKR apologist John Doerr said:

"There's no need to hold stubbornly to an outdated projection—strike it from your list and move on. Our goals are servants to our purpose, not the other way around."

Setbacks are normal in life and business. And, given our fast-paced world, course-correction is as common as course-plotting. The age-old saying: "nothing worth having ever comes easy" holds true here. So, when it comes to giving up, don't make any hasty decisions. Instead, regroup, and try to identify what's going wrong.

Here are four techniques that you (and your team) can use when dealing with a failed OKR Objective:

1. Reflect on the Problem

Whatever happened, happened.

Sure, it must feel awful, but there is nothing that you can do to change the past. Thinking about the setback in a negative way, and getting upset about it, will not help you achieve anything productive. However, if you take some time to consider all that has happened, then you can understand what went wrong, and provide your team with a better idea of how to prevent something similar from happening again.

Learning from your past mistakes is nothing to be ashamed of. In fact, if you can personally achieve some insight into what went wrong, then you can provide your team with the confidence they'll need—to overcome similar obstacles in the future.

2. Communicate

Keep your team in the loop.

It's ok to notify them of victories, as well as setbacks. Be cognizant of the size of your organization, and the extent of the setback. But work hard to ensure that your team is aware that they can trust you to provide them with honest and fair feedback.

Baseless rumors can blow an issue out of proportion. Everything that you think your team needs to know must directly come from you and no one else. If you address a setback openly, then it reduces the risk of unnecessary and baseless gossip and rumors.

And, it's not all about you. Let your team talk. Communication is a two-way street and you must keep the channels of communication open and honest, during such moments. That's important. But simple, honest communication after a setback is even more important. And, it signals to your team that one setback is not a failure that can break them.

3. Regroup

Reflection is important to move ahead. Dwelling on the past won't help you move forward. Once you clear the air about your current setback, then, it's time to re-energize the team and get going with your workflow. Negativity is contagious, so stay positive. You set the mood. If the team sees that their leader is able to stay positive even in the face of adversity, it will motivate them to do the same.

Every dark cloud has a silver lining, so find your silver lining and get going. Do something that will counteract the negatively charged environment, and help your team to de-stress, and move on.

One trick in handling failure, lies in having the foresight to prepare your team, before failure even strikes. An effective team understands the corporate vision. They have a shared goal and a shared responsibility, that motivates them to achieve their best, even when things are at their darkest.

So, talk to your team. Take them back to their roots, and tell them to remember why they were assembled in the first place. Give them a renewed sense of purpose, and get everyone back on track again.

4. Move Forward

You cannot change the past and you cannot predict the future. The only thing under your control is the present. So make the most of it. If it's time to lead your team in a new direction, then so be it. Do so with the same gusto you put to good use in previous fruitful projects. Remind your team of past successes, and trust them to continue along the journey. Motivate and inspire them—so that everyone can bounce back from the setback and land on their feet.

Common OKR Mistakes & Pitfalls

Let's talk about some of the most common OKR mistakes.

Mistake 1: Setting Unachievable and Uninspiring Objectives

Earlier in this book, we've encouraged you to set (what Andy Grove called) "stretch goals." These are very ambitious goals, which encourage your team to aim high.

But, one word of caution about "stretch goals:" It's possible to select lofty goals which only serve to frustrate your team. Or perhaps, on the day you set the goal, your team was not enthusiastically dedicated to its fulfillment anyway.

So, it's best to keep your "stretch goals" *just beyond* the threshold of attainability, but not too far beyond. Again, recall Andy Grove's quote: "70% is the new 100%."

Note that the rule does *not* say: "5% is the new 100%" or "10% is the new 100%." The rule is "70% is the new 100%" because, ultimately, your team has to perceive the goal as being (at least partially) in reach. The idea of setting OKRs is to challenge the employees in an organization to push harder and further; it isn't supposed to demotivate or frustrate them.

To avoid doing this, collaborate with your employees, set "stretch goals" together, but also set some goals that are slightly less challenging, and more attainable in the short term. So, even if your employees do not achieve 100% of a major goal, they can at least have the partial satisfaction of achieving substantial progress on a lesser goal.

If the employees start to feel like all of their objectives are "setup with the intent of total failure," then they might stop trying altogether. So there is a fine line to tread here and you must tread it carefully.

Mistake 2: Forgetting to appoint a DRI (Directly Responsible Individual)

In corporate lingo, D.R.I. stands for "Directly Responsible Individual."

And it means precisely what the name implies. There needs to be one person who can ensure that the OKRs are being looked after and pursued. In "OKR speak" this person is sometimes labeled the "OKR Champion." Practically speaking, he's usually a team leader or manager, who volunteers to keep track of team OKRs.

If the team is not assigned a DRI, then this can lead to a lack of discipline, and a lot of finger-pointing. So avoid this by assigning one person the task of monitoring the OKR metrics and progress reports on a regular basis.

This is very important when it comes to large teams, or during the first round of OKR implementation. Because you will inevitably have some team members who are not keen on participating. So it's best to have at least one OKR cheerleader on the floor.

Mistake 3: Creating too many OKRs.

You can make as many OKRs as you want. But if you want the OKRs to be effective, then you'd be wise to limit the number of OKRs you create per team. Typically you'd make between three to five.

Dumping too many tasks on any one employee will set him up for failure. Your team will lose focus, get overwhelmed, and might disengage from their work.

It's tempting to believe that setting numerous goals will incite a team to scurry faster. But when you set too many goals, especially incongruous goals, then OKRs can backfire. Sporadically multitasking, between various OKRs is not desirable behavior, and will reduce efficiency and productivity.

So remain cognizant of how many OKRs you're loading up your workers with. In the beginning, it's best to keep the number small. Of course, if you notice your team completing their OKRs too quickly, you can always add more (or increase the ambitiousness of the goals), later.

Mistake 4: Using vague language in your OKRs

Avoid using vague language in your OKRs—especially in your Key Results. Recall again, there are two parts to an OKR. There's the Objective, and there are the Key Results.

- The "Objective" is the future ambitious goal you want to achieve.
- And, the "Key Results" are the three or four distinct measurable tasks—which help gauge your progress—and tell you if you're on course to achieve your Objective.

An objective that simply states, "increase our sales" is ineffective and cannot be measured.

- What is the metric that would lead to increased sales?
- What is the percentage increase in sales, that you hope to see?
- What is the duration of time you'll require to achieve this objective?

If the OKRs are structured too vaguely, then it creates a lot of ambiguity and it becomes difficult for the employees to understand what is expected of them. You can avoid these problems by crafting your OKRs correctly the first time.

Mistake 5: Failing to track weekly OKR progress

One of the main reasons why OKRs are so effective is because they make it easy for managers to check on company-wide progress. The catch is, that managers must make it their duty to request weekly updates from their employees—thus ensuring that the OKRs are being attended to, and work is going smoothly.

If you only half-heartedly implement OKRs, and fail to check-in till the end of the quarter, you're likely to find that not much has been achieved. To avoid this, try to hold your team members accountable for regular (usually weekly) check-ins. If an organization is using OKRs for the first time, this is doubly important. Because you'll also need to check up on the efficiency of the OKRs themselves, and ask your employees for feedback on the value of the OKR framework.

Try to get your team members to aim for at least 10% completion per week, if you are using quarterly OKRs. And it's not just about checking-in weekly, there must also be a brief discussion of progress so that the employees feel like their efforts are being acknowledged.

Mistake 6: Refusing to allow good ideas to make it to the top

OKRs don't always have to flow from the top to the bottom. Some of the OKRs can flow from the bottom to the top as well.

If you exclusively create top-to-bottom objectives (without enough feedback from the employees), then this can have a negative effect on motivation and creativity. You must give a certain degree of autonomy to your employees to encourage free-thinking, innovation, and growth. So allow them to voice their opinions about the current OKRs in play.

Additionally, they should be able to develop their own OKRs, under the guidance of the team leader. And your OKR Champion can ensure that all his OKRs are harmonious with the goals established at the top. This can help to make the process of establishing OKRs a joint effort, and improves employee motivation.

Mistake 7: Failure to provide the right tools for the job

One of the worst mistakes a manager can make, is to crudely delegate an ambitious OKR, to a department that doesn't have the proper tools to complete it.

If you write out an OKR that would easily take 100 men to complete, and your team is composed of two people and an intern, then your staff probably won't be too happy about this task.

It's good to encourage your employees to think big. (This is why "stretch goals" are utilized in OKR.) But if you dump a task of this magnitude onto a department that is obviously ill-equipped to handle it, then, this will only create feelings of resentment and frustration among your employees.

If you are uncertain of exactly how many resources, or how much manpower is required, then just construct your OKRs with the proclamation that the Objectives are not "set in stone," and can be modified later, as more resources become available. Keep the lines of communication open with your team, and let your OKRs evolve, adapt, and grow with your company.

Ch. 7: Write your Company Vision Statement

In previous chapters, we've mentioned the importance of writing OKRs that are harmonious with your "company vision." But, surprisingly, we find that a lot of companies don't have much of a company vision at all. If your company is lacking in the "vision" department, then this chapter is for you. Successful leaders know that a shared vision is a powerful motivator. A compelling vision helps your team intuit the right course corrections, and it energizes your employees with a sense of purpose (and perhaps an enthusiastic rallying cry). If you want to motivate your team, to follow you through the daily corporate grind, you need to come up with a shared vision—that will inspire them to be (and do) their best.

Strive for clarity when conveying your vision

Fans of Mike Judge's HBO television series "Silicon Valley" are familiar with a running joke on the show. Each tech company that the characters encounter, has the same corporate vision. And that is :

"To change the world."

The joke resonates with tech workers because every company in Silicon Valley insists that their technology is about to "change the world"—no matter how petty or trite their invention actually is.

This is an example of a bad "Company Vision Statement."

For a more commonplace poorly-constructed Company Vision Statement, here's one from the non-profit charity "Goodwill Industries:"

"Every person has the opportunity to achieve his/her fullest potential and participate in, and contribute to, all aspects of life."

Now, this sounds like a noble sentiment. Achieving ones "fullest potential" and "participating in life" is a good thing I guess. But, as a vision statement, it tells you very little about what exactly Goodwill Industries has to do with any of it. Like so many company vision statements, this one sounds like a treatise on "How to achieve self-actualization through Buddhism." So, when you're laying out your team vision, try to avoid such ethereal taglines. Instead, choose a statement that conveys a more detailed and sober undertaking to the listener.

I like this Vision Statement from the **Boy Scouts of America**:

"To prepare every eligible youth in
America to become a responsible,
participating citizen and leader—who is
guided by the Scout Oath and Law."

Or, here's another good one from the **Leukemia & Lymphoma
Society**:

"To cure leukemia, lymphoma, Hodgkin's
disease, and myeloma, and improve the
quality of life of patients and their
families."

Notice how these last two statements leave little room for ambiguity. If you want to convey a solid corporate vision, then you must be clear with your goals, and your ultimate destination should not be open to interpretation.

Don't be afraid to dream big, and pursue lofty goals—that may take generations to complete. But, the clearer your statement is, the easier it will be for your employees to remain committed to its pursuit. As a rule of thumb, wordy vision statements, (as we saw in our Boy Scouts example) tend to contain more specificity. And, especially in the early days of a company, specificity should be preferred over poetic screeds.

When you can group together people with the same vision, the collective energy of the group will certainly catalyze. It fosters a real sense of commitment, and it ensures that success will have the same meaning for all those involved.

Give your employees a reason to get out of bed in the morning

At the end of the day, we all want our lives to have some sort of meaning. Fortunately, for us, existential meaning is highly subjective, and mappable onto multiple domains.

When your employees understand the reasons why they labor along your journey, then they'll experience a stronger sense of motivation to problem-solve, and figure out the best path for the team. If you can't manage to attach a sense of purpose to your employees' time, then you may find it difficult to inspire them to do their best work. And remember, "purpose" is subjective. Trying to define a purpose from your point of view, is possibly not comparable to their perspective.

This is why, with OKRs, we encourage feedback and public disclosure of goals, between the three levels of the corporation (from the employees to the managers and CEO). Remember how we stressed the importance of "goal harmony" in previous chapters?

If Team A is pursuing one goal, and Team B is pursuing an incompatible goal, and the outcome of both of these goals has nothing to do with the company Vision Statement, then this is when trouble happens. So work hard to foster a harmonious environment between the strata of your organizational hierarchy.

Make a separate "Life Goal Sketchbook"

I've noticed an interesting phenomenon that happens when I'm speaking to corporate teams about their OKRs. The meeting starts out in a typical fashion. I stand at the whiteboard, and layout some rules for creating OKRs. The employees will pick up on the system pretty quickly, and they promise to give it a try.

Then comes the part of the meeting where we start creating "company goals." And this is where I have to be careful. Because, if I let this meeting go on for too long, then the goals people choose tend to morph into goals of a more existential nature.

When people first initiate a goal-setting exercise, they'll start off by writing pragmatic goals, like:

"Increase our customer base by 25%."

But, as the meeting runs on into the night, something strange happens. They'll start choosing broader life goals like:

"I want more time off, so I can take my child to see his grandfather in France."

One must be careful to avoid mixing your life goals with your business objectives. This probably sounds obvious to you. But when I ask corporate teams to show me their goals, you'd be surprised with how often their personal goals are mixed in with their corporate goals. (And this applies to everyone—from interns to business owners.)

In the past, during an OKR training session, if a team member started jotting down too many ethereal life goals, then I'd have him erase them, and try to get him to focus on our OKR goals—for the company. Which, admittedly, tend to be (and indeed are designed to be) a bit more dry and pragmatic. But, after years of fighting this phenomenon, one day it occurred to me to simply embrace it. That is to say, when an employee starts mixing his life goals with his business goals, then, instead of tossing his life goals in the trashcan, I have him jot them down in a separate sketchbook. I call this the "Life Goal Sketchbook."

This has the benefit of allowing his mind to separate his personal life goals, from the corporate OKRs that we're working on.

In doing so, I want to convey to the employee that his personal life goals are important to him. And that they should indeed be written down somewhere, and even shared with his coworkers from time to time. But OKR goals are a separate animal, and they live in a different domain of rigid metrics and rules.

Now, with that said, one can never separate one's work life and personal life completely. Indeed, statistically, most American married couples met at work. So we would be wise to not ignore personal life goals completely in this book. Thus, we'll go over some tips so you can create your own "Life Goal Sketchbook." Remember, Life Goals are not OKRs. And your sketchbook is not a business plan.

Rather, your Life Goal Sketchbook is where you are free to do everything that *you cannot do*—during an OKR session. And, your Life Goal Sketchbook is (of course) quite distinct from your Company Vision Statement. In keeping these goals separate, we enable your brain to compartmentalize your goals, thus keeping your personal goals distinct from your corporate goals. There may be some overlap of course. But there is utility in remaining cognizant of the division. In your Life Goal Sketchbook, you are free to dream wildly about your future goals—at least for a little while.

I find that allowing for this alternate "exploratory goal-setting exercise," actually helps the employee to better structure his (more pragmatic) OKR goals. Because he's able to get his loftier personal goals down on paper, and this allows his conscious mind to accept that his life goal is, at least, in a safe holding pattern, whilst he attends to his more pressing OKR goals.

So let's describe what your "Life Goal Sketchbook" might look like.

There is an old self-help industry question that ponders:

"Are you striving to be your best self?"

This depends on what "best" means to you, and how you plan on achieving this elusive goal.

Goal-setting is the first step in our journey toward optimal self-actualization. But goal-setting is just a part of it. You can put considerable time and effort into figuring out your ideal goal, but if your attitude towards life (in general) is negative, then achieving your goal will be nearly impossible. Life is not all about what we know, nor what we plan for. It's about what we practice. And especially, "what we practice daily."

At the end of the day, your goals are about you. So do not worry (for even one minute) if your goal sounds crazy to other people. That's irrelevant. If your life goals don't scare you a little bit, you might have chosen the wrong life goals. And, as we all know, it's the crazy ideas that end up changing the world.

In a world wrought with dreary routine, goals give us a chance to dream.

Imagine you have a blank slate, and you can decide to draw anything you want on it. Don't worry about the obstacles immediately ahead. Just start sketching out your dreams first.

In your initial sketch, your goals do not have to be financial in nature.

What have you always wanted to do in life?

Start with the pleasurable possibilities, and then move on—to the more pragmatic ones.

When you're in the dreaming phase of the planning process, don't worry about the bills or mortgages. Instead, think about the ideal version of "you." Remember, this is just a preliminary exercise. You will have time to think more about the practicality of your dreams as you progress with your goal-setting.

As you start writing down your goals, you will begin to see the direction you want to head in, and this makes the process of decision-making easier. Let these initial (outlandish goals) serve as a preliminary benchmark, to your current more-pressing goals.

Feel free to use a paper journal, or even an artist's sketchbook to write down your goals. The medium isn't important. What's of utmost importance, is that you store all your goals somewhere.

Why?

Because you must come back to them later. As the years go by, you must return to them again, and again, and again.

Your life experience, motivations, and even your biochemistry will be different, each time you look at your goals. Ten, twenty, or thirty years from now, as you re-open this sketchbook of memories, some of the goals you scribe today, will seem completely ridiculous to you in the future. Other goals will seem so easy to do, that you'll be surprised you even bothered listing them as an objective.

Hopefully, at some distant point in the future, you will recognize some of your goals as being instrumental in changing your life for the better.

Feel free to keep your most intimate, or very long-term goals tucked away. But, for your more pragmatic daily goals, it's usually best to keep these in plain sight. Place a copy of your daily goals on your refrigerator or mirror. This will act as a constant reminder. And, repeated exposure to your goal aids in focusing your conscious (and subconscious mind) on what you want to achieve.

Be explicit when it comes to setting your life goals.

- Why is this goal so important to you?
- Is it important because your family wants you to do it, or because you want to?

For example, if your goal this year is to lose weight, then ask yourself why this is important to you? Will you take the necessary steps, and make the necessary sacrifices in attaining this goal?

The primary question that you must be able to answer is whether you will eventually feel a sense of achievement, when you achieve this goal or not.

For instance, suppose your goal is to become the best business in your niche market. But, you also really want to stay connected to your child, and coach your child's sports team. There will be times when achieving one goal, comes at the expense of another. And seeking harmony between all the goals in your sketchpad, is almost never possible.

Here are a couple of questions that you can ask yourself during your goal sketching exercise:

- What goals would I choose if I only had one year to live?
- What goals would I choose if I was sure I had 40 years to live?
- What would I do if I never had to worry about my finances again?
- What would I do if I was never afraid of failing?

Don't plan your entire life out in one day. Your goal-setting sketch pad is meant to be re-worked—throughout your life. Take at least a couple days to make big decisions. Sleep on them. Come back to them momentarily through the week. You'll find that, after a night of rest, goals tend to morph, and simply appear different—each time you look at them in the morning.

Throughout your life, you may have hundreds of goals. But there are only 24 hours in the day. So it's important to only pick three or four to concentrate on, at any given time. You don't have to do everything at once. Take it slow and steady. Once you've chosen a goal that is, not just important to you, but excites you as well, the next step is to start taking small steps that will help you in achieving your goal.

Stay away from the strategies that advocate an "all-or-nothing" approach. One small step a day can help you in achieving great results. Achieving Life Goals is a process, not a magic pill. You can create a one-step-a-day rule for yourself. This means that every day you will be doing something, regardless of how small or big it is, that will help you in achieving your goals.

However, give yourself a couple of "off days" as well. There are bound to be some days in which you haven't managed to make any progress toward your goal. That's okay. Don't be too hard on yourself. The more goals you make, the less time and energy you will have at your disposal for each one, so it will be wise to limit the number of goals you set for yourself. Indeed, perhaps one or two single Life Goals might be desirable, because it means that you will be able to dedicate all your time, energy, and focus towards a more narrow range of activities.

Ch. 8: Leadership & Team Development

Building (and maintaining) a team of dedicated, motivated employees, is the most challenging part of the business owner's (or manager's) job. It's difficult to find conscientious people— who *also* have an intrinsic desire to show up to work each morning. Additionally, the style by which a manager conducts his employees, varies from industry to industry. And, some *personality types* find some managerial styles, easier to execute than others. With that said, let's begin by describing the three most common types of managers we've encountered.

Three Different Management Styles

Style 1: The Visionary

A manager who is a Visionary, is good at conveying a "purpose" and a "direction" to his employees. They succeed when they convince their teams that the "vision" they have in mind, is valuable and important to the world. The Visionary often has their eyes set on the horizon, and thus, may find the day-to-day minutia of business to be tedious. Consequently, they might naturally avoid micromanaging employees. Which can be great for fostering autonomy. But, in keeping their eyes focused on the horizon, they may lose sight of the potholes directly in front of them. (For an excellent depiction of a Visionary gone mad, I highly recommend reading the best-seller "Bad Blood: Secrets and Lies in a Silicon Valley Startup" by John Carreyrou.)

Style 2: The Democracy

In a democratically run office, the majority rules (supposedly). Managers encourage employees to actively participate in corporate decisions. One upper-manager often has the "final say" on these decisions. But, because the employees are such active participants, they have a lot of influence. Team involvement and team preferences are highly valued in such schemas. Consequently such teams report a boost in morale and develop trust in relationships easily. Many employers (especially the "softie" type) prefer this sort of management style—even though they may never formally endorse it.

Because democratically run offices make "group decisions" this may remove some of the decision-making burden from the employer's shoulders. Thus, if any given decision goes wrong, the manager has the luxury of recounting that, indeed, the majority of the office voted on it. So it's not "all his fault."

Style 3: The Coach

Similar to your 4th period gym teacher Mr. Woodcock, some managers take on a coach-like persona. Such managers tend to be male, and are prone to engage in 5:00 pm chants—in which they loudly exclaim the many virtues of Burlington Toiletries, or whatever their product might be.

Some employees seem to find all this to be entertaining, some find it annoying, and some find to be just downright bizarre. But, depending on your industry, this management style is quite popular, and may be effective, especially in sales.

Which style is right for you?

Only you can decide which managerial style will work best for your personality, and for your industry. There are pros and cons to each persona. And most managers will have to wear all three hats, at one time or another.

The Art of Office Communication

Communication is key.

As a business owner or manager, the majority of your day will be spent communicating with team members. So understanding the nuances that dictate how humans communicate has obvious benefit. Recall the CEO joke again—the acronym CEO usually stands for "Chief Email Officer."

Below, we've listed five important communication skills that *effective* managers utilize.

#1. Treat your employees like human beings

In corporate speak, there is a tendency to use the words "we" or "us" or say things like, "the company feels..." But when you're talking to your employees, speak to them as individuals, and avoid the natural tendency to use the "royal we." Your company may have many cogs in many wheels. But, ultimately, the clockwork of your company is composed and maintained by people—in all their sheer brilliance and absurdity. So embrace this notion, and accept the curious proclivities of the human tapestry.

#2. Let the people come to you

As a manager, you have to be a problem solver. But if you don't have an open-door policy then you may never know what problems need your attention. So try not to close yourself off from your team. You can participate in the daily grind with them, while still maintaining an air of authority.

When possible, encourage them to solve problems themselves. This entails dispensing some degree of trust and authority —to each position in the company. You'll find that your enterprise works best when it has, not one problem-solver, but dozens—all working towards the same goal, autonomously.

#3. Listen when giving directions

Most managers make the mistake of believing that their instructions are crystal clear upon delivery. Primarily because, the directions indeed *are* crystal clear —in the manager's mind. The delivery of instructions via words is a messy psychological process. And conveying information, especially complex technical information, is necessarily error-prone.

So when you're talking to your employees, listen to their responses, and watch their body language. Ask for feedback when appropriate, and listen to their concerns. As Stephen Covey famously wrote in "The 7 Habits of Highly Effective People:"

"Seek first to understand, then to be understood."

#4. Use notes and a Call-to-Action

As a team leader, it's important that you maintain *some idea* about which objective each team member is working toward. OKRs excel at tracking medium-range tasks. But for those times when rapid-fire instructions are being dispersed quickly, a different sort of communication is required.

One in which instructions are doled out in the heat of the moment. If you tell an employee to do something and you don't see that employee writing it down somewhere, then there is a fair chance that it will never get done. Moreover, keeping your own notes is usually essential in following up.

Now, I take notes on everything. There are thousands of lists and checklists in my PC, which outline everything from how to launch a software app, to how to wash the car. (For a great discussion on the power of checklists, read "The Checklist Manifesto" by Dr. Atul Gawande.) But, that said, I have worked with many teams (consisting of both managers and employees) who are simply *not* note-takers. They just don't like them. And for such people, there's nothing I can say to convince you to scribe out some sort of task-tracking note. So, I won't try too hard here. But if you are one of those managers who arrives at the office each morning, and is completely shocked to learn that the majority of tasks have not been completed, then consider spending a day with a pad and pencil, and simply noting down tasks, as you dispense them.

Most importantly, it's helpful to end your conversations with a Call-to-Action. In marketing, a Call-to-Action is a blurb of copy that prompts the reader on —to their next action step—typically to buy a product or signup to a website. So, when you're interacting with your employees, try to end your conversations with a mini Call-to-Action. That is to say, when an interaction is coming to an end, then take a moment to sum up what was just discussed. Particularly, have the employees restate what deliverable is to be rendered, and when will it be revealed.

#5. Avoid Anger

As a leader, you have to be the rock.

Office politics and emotions often run high, and result in destructive or pugnacious behavior among your employees. But emotional outbursts are almost never the solution. As the French essayist Joseph Joubert wrote:

"The aim of argument, or of discussion, should not be victory, but progress."

Remember, failure is common. And failing forward is essential for remaining competitive—especially in this fast-paced (technologically-enabled) 21st-century business environment. Allowing the malaise of failure to linger within your department is detrimental to your success. So remain stoic, when things go awry. Don't argue. Just keep moving forward. In "How to Win Friends and Influence People" Dale Carnegie famously wrote:

"...I have come to the conclusion that there is only one way...to get the best of an argument - and that is to avoid it. Avoid it as you would avoid rattlesnakes and earthquakes. Nine times out of ten, an argument ends with each of the contestants more firmly convinced than ever, that he is absolutely right.

You can't win an argument. You can't because if you lose it, you lose it; and if you win it, you lose it. Why? Well, suppose you triumph over the other man and shoot his argument full of holes… Then what? You will feel fine. But what about him? You have made him feel inferior. You have hurt his pride. He will resent your triumph. And [as the old adage states:] "A man convinced against his will, Is of the same opinion still."

How to be a Leader

Leading your team to success can (sometimes) feel a bit like herding cats. If you start yelling and screaming, you're just going to startle them. Instead, you have to make them interested in walking down the same path that you're walking down. In many ways, this is the primary role of a good leader.

In this section, we'll list five important leadership characteristics.

#1. Good leaders are organized

If you want your company to be organized, then organization starts with you. In the previous section, we stressed the need for maintaining checklists, task-tracking, and logging employee directions. Your ability to successfully perform such daily *Information Management* chores, is pivotal in your performance as a manager.

More important than any complex digital system, or elaborate GPS tracking circuitry, if you can manage to merely maintain a day-planner of meetings and acquaintances, then you're probably doing better than most managers we've met. Successfully shuffling your body around, from one corporate huddle to the next, often occupies the majority of managerial efforts. As Woody Allen said:

"Showing up is 80% of life."

#2. Good leaders have Emotional Intelligence

Being a good leader almost necessarily entails having a good grip on Emotional Intelligence. The term Emotional intelligence encompasses a set of skills like:

- Being able to identify or predict which emotions will arise in your employees.
- The capacity to recognize your own emotions, to discern between them, and label them correctly.
- The ability to curtail your own negative emotions, and remain calm under pressure.
- And, the ability to calibrate your current emotional palette —to suit the needs of whichever environment you find yourself in.

Striving to remain cognizant of our inner drives, and the vacillating emotions of your team members, is beneficial for good management and leadership. As Alexander Pope wrote in 1733:

Know then thyself, presume not God to
scan;
The proper study of mankind is man.
Plac'd on this isthmus of a middle state,
A being darkly wise, and rudely great.

#3. Good leaders know their industry

We shouldn't have to tell you that, as a manager, "knowing your
industry" is important. But as many who have had any experience
in corporate America already know, often, the employees know
the business better than the manager. There are a variety of
reasons for this. Primarily being because managers are often hired
because of their prior management skills —that were often
honed in another industry. Perhaps one that is far removed from
the industry in which they currently find themselves. If this is the
case, then this doesn't mean that you should take refuge, by
delegating industry-specific knowledge to underlings. Rather you
should work hard to learn every aspect of your industry, listen to
your employees, and have them bring you up to speed.

#4. Good leaders set the pace and the tone

Remember, with OKR, we like to keep our expectations high.
Pursuing lofty, almost unachievable goals, is par for the course in
OKR. But keeping expectations high (in general) should be the
default state in your office. Maintaining a high bar for daily

output, ensures that you maintain a high level of yearly productivity.

On a typical crew team, the most technically-capable rower is positioned at the bow of the boat. This role is special, because the man occupying this seat, will set the pace for the entire crew of rowers.

As a manager, it is your job to occupy this position. Your team will mimic the pace you set. If you approach your job in a haphazard and lackadaisical fashion, then your team will too. If you respect yourself, take your position seriously, and engage in ambitious daily action, then your team will feel more inclined to model themselves after your example.

#5. Good leaders are consistent (The "just-world hypothesis")

People appreciate fairness and consistency. It makes us feel safe and secure, to know that *bad actions* have consequences, and *good actions* get rewarded.

We all want to believe in the "Just-World Hypothesis." It's a cognitive bias which posits that any person's good deeds will (ultimately) be rewarded. And his bad deeds will be punished (at least someday).

The Just-World Hypothesis is a fallacy of course. But that doesn't matter. As a manager, it's your job to make sure that the Just-World Hypothesis exists—at least on your office floor from Monday through Friday.

If you can reliably treat your employees with *fairness and consistency*, this helps build trust, confidence, and respect. But, if your behavior is erratic and unpredictable, and you are prone to emotional outbursts, then this creates employee anxiety, and doubt. Nobody wants to work for Dr. Jekyll and Mr. Hyde.

The Top 3 Leadership Mistakes

You're a manager, so that means you're a problem solver. But wouldn't it be nice if every employee in your department was also a problem solver. Depending on your industry, you might be in a position to actually make this happen. In the majority of offices we encounter, most employees can be doing much more independent problem-solving than they're currently doing.

Below, we've listed three attributes that often hinder autonomous employee problem-solving in a typical office.

Problem 1: Too much micromanaging

If you run the kind of office where people need to sign-in before they open the refrigerator, this will probably not be conducive to the fostering of an environment in which your employees man-up, and take the reins (when appropriate).

So, don't be afraid to delegate work to an underling. Most people will rise to the challenge, if you let them, and if they can see that their particular field of expertise is needed to help the team. Don't hover over your employee's shoulders. Don't second-guess their intermediate decisions. Obsessive micromanaging will frustrate even the most patient of employees.

Problem 2: Your employees are afraid to offer suggestions.

In business, it is typical to be faced with two competing proverbs:

"The squeaky wheel gets the grease."

---

and

"The nail that sticks out gets hammered down."

We might take the first proverb as indicating that the employee who makes noise, gets listened to. The second proverb, is a warning against attempts to shun conformity. As a manager, things typically go best when you are able to find some sort of middle ground. Specifically when you foster an environment in which beneficial suggestions have an avenue by which they can percolate up to the top.

Problem 3: Chiding your employees for taking risks and making mistakes

Employees at Google are encouraged to dedicate 20% of their time to working on their own pet projects. Obviously, the vast majority of these side projects never make any money for Google. If anything, the majority of these projects are costing Google millions of dollars per year. Because 20% of the workweek amounts to nearly two months of labor cost per employee. But when you realize that Gmail, Google Maps, Twitter, Slack, and Groupon all started as "side projects" then their utility makes more sense.

So if you're the kind of manager that yells at an employee for spending a dollar more to buy Snapple instead of Coke, then you might be creating an environment in which your employees are afraid to try anything new at all.

Team Building 101: How to attract (and keep) top talent

Take the hiring process very seriously.

It is sometimes estimated that 3/4 of all new hires have been "mismatched" in their new role. They end up being the wrong person for the job. This could be bad in monetary terms, but it can also be costly to company morale, office productivity, and psychological cohesion.

If you've ever tried to recruit talent, especially in a technical domain, then you know how difficult this process can be. The current job market favors the rare high-IQ bird. And these people often already know that they are in demand. Working to attract the high-quality applicants entails learning how to differentiate your company, from other organizations in your industry. Below, we will list some ways to try to make this happen.

#1. Be clear in who you are and what you need

The first step in recruiting new talent, is to be clear in communicating three things:

1. What you're looking for.
2. What you're willing to pay.
3. And, what your company's mission is.

In the "game of love" the easiest way to attract a desirable mate, is to simply be desirable yourself. This method works for your human resources department too. Selling your company as an "attractive work environment" is a whole lot easier, if your company *actually is* an attractive work environment.

Find ways to authentically express your goals —be that via your company website, videos, or branding. But, even more importantly, (as you're probably aware) most business relationships are established because of *tertiary networks*—i.e. when someone introduces you to "a friend of a friend," and this person becomes your new hire, new trading partner, or new CFO.

Because of this phenomenon, your current employees are necessarily ambassadors for your brand. Each time they interact with somebody (in a bar, or tradeshow, or Skype call), they are (in part) representing your company. So, keeping these employees happy, and incentivizing them to provide hiring recommendations, is definitely in your interest.

#2. Take retention seriously

Losing good people means losing money.

So work hard to monitor your employee's mood and morale. If there are any unhappy employees among you, then strive to see why this is so. Perhaps you can alter the environment or the team dynamics —so that this person is satisfied.

Indeed, losing a conscientious employee (that is even moderately successful in his position) is extremely costly —even if you do manage to quickly find someone "better." This is particularly true, when we're talking about unquantifiable costs—like the cultural and emotional cost to your team, and the risk involved when introducing new members to an already-established group.

#3. Build on the strengths of your employees

Each employee has a unique set of skills and traits. More importantly, each employee has one aspect of their job that they genuinely enjoy doing. So work hard to try to match the right employee with the right task. Getting to know your employees and taking note of their skills, preferences, and personal background, is pivotal here. Each person on your team will bring their own prejudices and perspectives to the table. So, as a manager, it is your job to synergize this multitude of viewpoints, and get everyone to work together, toward the collective good.

Also, be ready to source new leaders from within your own team. Leaders are usually not born, they are made. Every leader starts somewhere. So perhaps one is being forged in the fires of your main office, right this minute.

#4. Offer continual education & mentorship programs

Intelligent people in sophisticated positions (especially in tech), are in a continual state of learning. So facilitating this process makes your organization more attractive. High-performing people understand that there is more to a job, than the monthly salary. There is an ancillary benefit in being able to improve upon a skillset or do novel research. And the more innovative your company, the more you are apt to capitalize on this phenomenon. As the great American physicist Richard Feynman said:

"When you do something the first time, you're a scientist. When you do something the second time, you're an engineer. And, when you do something the third time, you're just a technician."

Meaning that, the most talented among us often, don't like to be technicians. They like to be working on something new and novel. So strive to tailor the employee experience so that there are many opportunities for exploration and intellectual growth.

The traditional mentorship model is a bit of an anachronism in the modern age. This is unfortunate, because it's an excellent form of information conveyance. And, most great leaders can rattle off the names of various mentors in their lives. So strive to foster an environment in which mentorship is encouraged and welcomed.

#5. Be flexible with schedules and compensation

It may be necessary to offer new employees a unique compensation package, as well as an unconventional time schedule. For candidates that are particularly in-demand, you may have to wrap your schedule around *them*, rather than the other way around. Depending on your industry, being inflexible on this issue may (or may not) be warranted. But just be advised that inflexible work hours (particularly in the digital age), are often a sticky point for in-demand tech hires.

#6. Beware of envy, pride, and greed

If you are blessed with the thrill of managing particularly intelligent team members, or if you're managing a team of upwardly mobile professionals, then, do not make the mistake of perceiving their forward momentum as a threat.

Competing with your own team is the fastest way to lose their respect, and the fastest way to turn your workplace into a toxic environment.

The best leaders are the ones that genuinely care for each member of their team. And, sometimes, this might even be at the expense of the leader's own personal or professional goals. It is this sort of "sacrifice for the team" that is the hallmark of great leadership. As Simon Sinek likes to say:

"Poor leaders will sacrifice the people to save the numbers.
Great leaders are willing to sacrifice the numbers to save the people."

Ch. 9: Stimulate Employee Motivation

It is your duty to motivate your team. If you are a manager or a boss, then *you* are your team's coach and cheerleader. And your team members will look to you for critique, guidance, and support. A highly motivated group of people is the best asset a business can have. In this section, we'll talk about what it takes to motivate your team.

About Human Motivation

Human motivation is a funny thing. If you were to only listen to the great capitalist of old, you might think that the "mechanisms of motivation" were quantified long ago. And that, merely adopting a "carrots and sticks" strategy is enough to induce your employees to keep showing up each morning for the daily grind—during which they endure great physical or cognitive labor, all in the pursuit of their own selfish interests.

Well, if you thought that the "almighty dollar" was the primary impetus behind your employee's motivation, then you might want to listen up. Some experiments on incentives, actually show that, as the monetary reward increases, cognitive performance decreases. The reason for this is not clear. But the role of financial incentive seems to be secondary to other social dynamics—like **Autonomy, Mastery, and Purpose**. Let's discuss each of these motivators briefly.

Motivator 1: Autonomy

"Autonomy" describes our desire to lead a self-directed life. It entails the freedom to choose from an array of options, of daily activities. The *number and quality* of options presented to us are particularly important, when these options are about "career choices." Employees with "high autonomy" are given more freedom in corporations, and are sometimes encouraged to select the projects that they find most interesting to work on.

Motivator 2: Mastery

"Mastery" is about the inner urge one feels, to nurture a skill. Curiously, we seem to experience joy when mastering a complex task, even if the completion of this task will have absolutely no positive benefit to our lives. Anyone who has ever become enraptured with a videogame, is well aware of this experience. We know that becoming proficient in Super Mario Brothers will not increase our standing in life. It won't improve our resume, make us more popular with the opposite sex, nor put food on the table. And yet, we play, and play, and play. We spend long hours mastering these games, for reasons unknown to us. Other than the fact that, at the time, we just "think it's fun." Wouldn't it be great if your employees felt this way about their jobs too?

Motivator 3: Purpose

"Purpose" entails the desire to do activities that are valuable and meaningful. Activities that are meaningful to yourself, meaningful to your family, or meaningful to humanity in general. When the brain perceives a goal as having real value, then it will encourage your conscious mind to progress along the steps that would enable you to accomplish this goal. However, when your brain doesn't see the immediate value (in whatever you're working on), then it may attempt to discourage you from the task. It will introduce boredom, doubt, insecurity, and despair to your conscious mind. And you'll lose your "mojo." You just won't *feel* very inspired to do the task at hand. The more questionable the value of the task, the less you'll want to do it.

It's this sort of "punishment and reward" system that kept your ancestors alive.

Here's a thought experiment to understand this phenomenon. Suppose a wealthy land baron told you that a $100 dollar bill was buried someplace in his massive 500-acre property. And if you dug a 10-foot hole, at a randomly selected location, then you just might find it. Now, if your brain is working correctly, it should discourage you from this undertaking. This pursuit has a very high cost, and a very low probability of garnering any reward at all. Even if you were to start this task, your brain would discourage you from completing it, during the entire digging process. As it should.

Now, consider the same scenario, except this time our wealthy land baron says he'll give you a million dollars for digging one 10-foot hole. Getting that amount of money for just a couple hours of labor is an obviously beneficial pursuit. And, though the labor required in this scenario is the same as it was in the previous scenario, the emotions that your brain will present to your conscious mind, will be much different. Your brain will encourage you to do the task, and to work quickly and diligently—all in pursuit of the massive million-dollar payoff.

Note that one need not use money as the primary motivator in our thought experiment. Instead of one million dollars, suppose the land baron offered you the "cure for cancer" in exchange for your labor, or the formula for cold fusion, or a date with a supermodel, or a chance to meet the president. The nature of the reward is not important. What's important is that our laborer thinks that the reward has value *to him*.

Build a "motivator-rich" work environment

So how do we encourage intrinsic motivation in our employees?

The solution lies in, first, understanding the difference between intrinsic and extrinsic motivation. If you are coerced into doing something, (like lift weights for an hour at gunpoint) then, this is an example of extrinsic motivation—because the motivating force is external to your mind. But if you elect to exercise because you *personally* seek a better, healthier physique, and you drag yourself to the gym each morning to get it, then this is an example of *intrinsic motivation.*

Our three above-described attributes (of Autonomy, Mastery, and Purpose) all make up the magic *cocktail* that brings forth *intrinsic motivation* in your workforce. How your organization works to foster these three traits will depend on factors that are unique to your business. No two companies have the same corporate schema, and only you will know which methods will work best. But, with that said, we'll list some general principles now.

#1: Make sure your employees know why they are valuable

As a manager (or business owner), the value of any given employee may be obvious to you. But, often, the value of the job may not be obvious to the employee himself. So, to get the best work out of each employee, strive to instill a sense of "purpose, value, and meaning," into each position on the corporate ladder. This might entail something as simple as showing your employee exactly how his work output affects other employees in the corporate works. Even if the job in question entails crude physical labor or monotonous drudgery, this doesn't mean that a *sense of purpose* and value cannot be gleamed from it.

Consider common wartime depictions of army medics. or grunts—running gallantly through dangerous, conditions (on a war-torn battlefield), to help save a fallen comrade. This job is anything but stylish. In fact, it's the dirtiest and scariest job a person can do. And yet, the medic feels intrinsically motivated to do it. Because he knows his team needs him, and he immediately sees the obvious value—that he is in a position to provide.

#2: Be transparent

Throughout this book, we've tried to stress the importance of "transparency" in applying the OKR framework. Indeed, part of the effectiveness of OKR relies upon the *open manner* in which OKRs are assigned to various members of an organizational hierarchy. This can be of particular importance when motivating employees because, each employee is able to see how the output of their (seemingly) inconsequential job, actually percolates up, to the higher levels of the organization, and (ultimately), to the construction of the final product.

Remember, people experience *intrinsic motivation* when they see "purpose, value, and meaning" in their work. And you encourage these emotions when you keep your organization transparent to allow your employees to see why their job is valuable.

#3: Encourage employee self-development and continual education

You offer value to employees when you provide them with opportunities for personal growth. This might entail mentorship, skillset growth, physical wellness, or even intellectual or social self-development. What's important is that the employee perceives his life as *improving* each day that he is employed by you.

#4: Invite group feedback and collaboration

The majority of people, in any given organization, feel that their input isn't appreciated. If a person feels like they're not valued, then they may withdrawal from contributing altogether. You don't want this. So, encourage employee participation and (especially) employee anonymous feedback, when possible. And, acknowledge the good suggestions you receive, regardless of whether you implement them or not.

#5: Keep an open-door policy

An "open-door policy" is typically encouraged. Specifically, individual employees need to believe that they can trust you if they walk in your office and surrender information. This is not to say that your office should be a fount of gossip-mongering, nor a priest's confessional. But it does mean that work-related items can be freely discussed in private. There is great value in discretion here. It's important to maintain these environments because a critique of other employees is often best done in private.

#6: Try to keep em' happy

Each employee is born with a different level of baseline happiness. And people who appear unhappy, actually might be quite content. But, generally speaking, a happy employee is a productive employee. Happiness (and a daily positive attitude) are contagious. So, ensure that you take the necessary steps to keep up employee morale.

#7: Be generous in rewarding little victories

Recall that, with OKR, we set "stretch goals." (Goals that are impossible to fully achieve, because the initial goal itself is so ambitious.) But this doesn't mean you should ignore *little victories*—especially at the employee level.

While it's good to keep pushing your staff to move beyond their preconceived limits, one must also be careful not to let their successes go by unrecognized. Just as the rat in a maze will be encouraged to keep running, after smelling increasingly bigger wafts of cheese, so too are humans obliged to keep working, when they see their labor being appreciated, utilized, and celebrated.

#8: Use custom-tailored employee reward packages

When you're considering rewarding employees, remember that people want different things, at different stages of their lives. So, try to remain cognizant of varying tastes and preferences. For example, an *all-expenses-paid* trip to Cancun might sound wonderful for the younger folks in your company, but might have limited appeal for employees who are on the verge of retiring. Incentive packages tend to work the best when there are at least three options to choose from. So, besides the "Cancun trip," consider adding an alternate prize.

#9: Use ceremony to acknowledge over-achievers

As cheesy as it may sound, electing an "employee of the month" actually works. You don't have to put a cheaply framed portrait on the wall. But conducting a ritual in which an employee (or group of employees), are publicly honored for exceptional work, actually does help to motivate your workforce. Indeed, receiving a public acknowledgment from your peers is often the greatest source of intrinsic motivation.

The thrill of victory will flee rapidly, if you don't work to devise *some* sort of ceremony to catch it. As the Duke of Wellington remarked at the Battle of Waterloo:

"...nothing, except a battle lost, can be half so melancholy as a battle won."

After your team succeeds in passing a *major* milestone, take a moment to *stop*, and acknowledge each member's role. There will always be more work to do later. And, by their very nature, corporate visions are never complete. So the war will always be there waiting for you tomorrow.

Thus, whenever your team accomplishes a goal, strive to make it readily obvious to everyone, how "the completion of this goal" positively affected the team's climb up the mountain. This form of positive reinforcement provides team members with a sense of accomplishment and confidence. Again, this is why the OKR framework is so rich. Because progress is judged in quarterly

victories, and Key Result metrics provide objective milestones—
that display employee accomplishments to their peers.

Ch. 10: Employee Performance Reviews

All of us in the corporate world have (at one time or another) sat through a performance review meeting. Perhaps you were the one conducting the review, or perhaps you were the victim sitting across the desk—in a state of Dilbertian terror. Unfortunately, most performance reviews, though good-intentioned, are usually poorly executed. In fact, it's fair to say that the majority of reviews conducted in the majority of corporations, probably do more harm than good.

With that said, in this chapter, we're going to try to layout a more productive process that might make employee review sessions a bit more bearable and fruitful.

Employee Prep.

Every corporation has a unique format for conducting employee performance reviews. But, whichever format you choose, it's of utmost importance that your new employees are not surprised by the questions, during their first review session. So, well before the meeting, present your employees with an outline, detailing how performance reviews are conducted, and what will be expected of them during the interview.

It's also helpful for the employee to be familiar with which metrics will be used to gauge their quarterly performance. Unfortunately, even in a best-case scenario, such metrics are often quite ethereal. And employee behavior and performance is difficult to quantify. You may be tempted to employ OKR metrics in this review session. But, as we have cautioned earlier in this book, using OKR Objectives (or other goal-setting frameworks), for employee performance review metrics, might not be fruitful. Because the completion of OKR goals is often dependent on factors that are out of the employee's control— like the actions of other members on his team, external market forces, or even luck.

Manager Prep.

As a manager, it's your job to pre-prep for the conversation with the employee. If you go into such interviews and "play jazz," then these sessions will be less fruitful, and you may miss an important chance for *feedback and reinforcement*. Most importantly, review sessions are an opportunity to encourage your employees on their path to further success, *and* to congratulate them as well—for past work accomplishments.

If you are new to conducting employee reviews sessions, then it's often best to act out a review session with a colleague. Pretend that you are the employee and he is the boss. And then, switch it up. You play the employee and let him be the boss. By mimicking a review session from both sides of the desk, this will give you unique insight into the perspective of both parties. Take notes along the way. And, when you are finally ready to conduct the actual employee review session, it's often useful to have a brief outline of four or five points that you want to discuss during the meeting.

Remember to try to always end on a positive tone. But, most importantly, the last point in your outline should entail some sort of action step—that is to be accomplished in the *next quarter* by the employee.

Don't hold in praise or criticism till the last moment

Have you ever heard an employee say:

"This is the first time anyone has told me about this!"

It is important that the employee review session itself, not be the absolute first time that an employee has experienced praise, nor critique. If it is, then he will likely be emotionally taken aback in a positive or negative direction. And jarring his neurophysiological state in this fashion will hamper your ability to engage in effective discourse.

Ideally, praise and critique should be dispensed when appropriate throughout the workweek. Such that, by the time the performance review session actually happens, it should merely stand as a review of matters already discussed, and only emphasize the most pivotal points.

The Art of Conversation

Maintaining a healthy conversational attitude throughout a performance review is desirable and beneficial to clear communication. The attitude and mood (set by you) throughout this meeting is critical for fluid discourse, from start to finish. Most importantly, the employee has to actually trust that you are indeed looking out for his best interests, and that you genuinely want to improve his status in the company. And that you're not merely playing corporate politics, nor critiquing his inadequacies.

If you find that *you* are doing all the talking, or if the meeting starts to sound like an insurance seminar or college lecture, then the performance review is probably not going well.

Remember, happy employees make for more profitable companies. So the performance review might be a game of brinkmanship in which *both* the positive *and* negative aspects of the job are discussed; but (after which) *both* parties leave the room with a commitment to positive, productive change.

To encourage more dialogue during your meeting, here are some conversation-starters to get the employee talking:

- Question 1: What are the primary goals you wish to achieve with this company in the next 12 months?

- Question 2: Which task do you think will be the most challenging next quarter?
- Question 3: Is there anything that this department can do for you, that would make it easier for you to accomplish this task?
- Question 4: During a typical work month, how many times would you like to receive feedback?
- Question 5: Do you currently feel like you are being micromanaged, or do you wish that you had more autonomy in your position?
- Question 6: What can *I do* to be a better manager?

Evaluate the quarter, not the week

During performance review sessions, there is a natural tendency to focus on the last two or three weeks of events in the office. But, this is not what a performance review should be about. Rather, you are supposed to be reviewing the performance of the employee in the entire quarter.

So, just try to remain cognizant of the fact that your brain may be biased to color your quarterly performance review by *recent events*, rather than events that happened months ago. This is why it is beneficial to keep an informal log of positive and negative attributes about the employee's performance, each month. So that, by the time you actually sit down for your discussion, your meeting will be less about what happened last Tuesday, and more about the multitude of events on the piece of paper in front of you.

Try to be positive

When meeting with an employee, some managers have a tendency to jump right into a line-by-line critique of job performance. While this is obviously important, one must be careful to not let *negativity* overwhelm the entire meeting. Remember, employees are people too. They have emotions and defensive reflexes—which may kick in, even when presented with logically-delivered criticism. This point is obvious to some, but not so obvious to others—as anyone who has worked in a department full of computer engineers can attest to.

So keep things positive. It's important that future review sessions are not dreaded by employees (year after year). Foster an environment of positive feedback, and focus on how the employee can continue to grow, what obstacles the employee has already successfully overcome, and what aspects of the employee's work you personally find most admirable.

Try to use sentences like this:

"I was personally really impressed with how you handled the Ginsberg account."

Not like this:

"The company benefited from the way you handled the Ginsberg account."

The first sentence is much more personable, and adds a human flare to the interaction.

What to do when things go bad

Performance reviews get tricky when you have an employee whose performance has simply not been very good. Often, there is no easy way to handle such cases. And the way you *do* handle it will depend on factors unique to the issue and unique to your organization.

Firing an employee is sometimes the only option. But, performance review sessions, are typically not the place to discuss such things. If there are some areas that need improvement, don't shy away from mentioning them. Try to speak directly, and stick to the point, in an effort to acknowledge problems and advise solutions. Wimpy managers (managers who really hate conflict), try to avoid dishing out criticism. But, if you attempt to skirt around the issue, and you're not direct enough, then an employee may fail to comprehend the gravity of the situation. And, this won't be helpful for anyone. Remember the point of these meetings is to actually promote growth, not mask problems that need to be addressed.

Ask for Feedback

Try to obtain feedback from the employee's peers or colleagues. Particularly from colleagues that have worked closely with the employee for some time. It's best to do this in private of course. And don't use too much time during one employee's performance review session, to ask about another employee. Try to gather information about colleagues during other, more informal and nonconsequential interactions.

Listening to your employee, and working to absorb and manifest his suggestions, are the traits of a good manager. And, when performance reviews are done correctly, they can enhance your relationships. And, hopefully, your performance reviews will indeed, actually succeed in improving the performance of your team.

Common Mistakes

With the above in mind, let's take a moment to list some of the typical mistakes that managers make, when conducting employee reviews.

Mistake #1: Don't use a performance review session as an opportunity to engage in employee training, employee coaching, or as an opportunity to discuss a salary increase.

You can conduct meetings for salary compensation, or for employee development. But if you attempt to mix the two, then this is usually not desirable.

It's often best, to keep discussions of money out of the entire review process (unless, you are actually conducting the review for this very purpose).

The biggest problem with trying to merge *employee compensation* discussions with *employee development* discussions, lies in the fact that, if the employee thinks money is *on the table*, then they may be transfixed by this notion. As my old boss used to say:

"Money makes people funny."

You don't want to let the hint of financial reward color the way your employee responds to important review questions.

Mistake #2: Don't have a manager (who does not work with the employee each week), conduct the review session.

Obviously, nobody wants to sit down and discuss complicated corporate topics, with somebody whose work life is far removed from the day-to-day of the job. Unfortunately, corporations sometimes have a bad habit of appointing *one person* to make the rounds to *several* different departments—to access employee aptitude. Often, this interloper has limited knowledge of daily operations and may be inquiring about things he knows absolutely nothing about. So, obviously, when you're laying out your corporate review hierarchy, try to avoid such predicaments, and get input from immediate managers.

Mistake #3: Don't surprise the employee during a Monday morning at 8:00 a.m., and tell him that "his performance review is today."

Give the employee advanced warning about the *date and time* of his review session. And tell him what will be expected of him. This allows people time to gather documents and stats. But, more importantly, it gives employees time to mentally prepare for the meeting.

Mistake #4: Don't be vague in your feedback.

Some organizations give performance feedback in the form of numerical metrics, or even letter grades. While these things are not bad in and of themselves, if the only thing an employee can see on his report card is a "C-," then this can be disquieting.

Moreover, brief numerical values, and vague one-liner sentences, may be clear to the person conducting the employee review. But when hiring managers (or human resources departments) come across this data in the future, they won't have any background information depicting why the scores were given.

So work hard to develop a more thorough system for grading performance. One that is clear to the employee, to the manager conducting the review, and even to future managers (or higher-ups), who may look at this data in years to come.

Mistake #5: Don't disregard problems that your employee brings up, only to put them off until next quarter.

Managers tend to be good at writing problems down, during review sessions. But, unfortunately, this is often the extent to which employee issues are ever followed up on.

If there is a reason why an employee (or department) is faltering, then review sessions should (ideally) tease these out. Strive to get employees to discuss perceived problems. And, instead of merely logging their issues, try to arrive at some sort of solution. This is not always possible of course. But be cognizant of the natural tendency to prefer to "pass the buck"—down to the next manager, in the next quarter, or in the next year.

Mistake #6: Don't evaluate personal quirks or traits. Evaluate behaviors and results.

Every employee comes packaged with different personal habits and traits, as well as differing opinions on leadership, motivation, and conscientiousness. Also, the external attitude that an employee displays to other employees may vary dramatically. Not every person in the world is designed to have the charisma of a self-development speaker (à la Tony Robbins), nor the oration skills of Barack Obama.

People are *different*, of course.

Indeed, if you are used to working with technically capable, or highly intelligent people, you'll notice that they're often rather withdrawn and introverted. And many of them have quirky (often charming), little behaviors and routines. Working with the idiosyncrasies of your fellow humans, is part of The Human Experience. And your employee review sessions are not the time to try to stomp these traits out. Instead, try to focus on behaviors that have been observed directly last quarter, particularly on the positive results your employee was able to accomplish.

Ch. 11 How to Run an Effective Meeting

The majority of topics discussed in the workplace, typically don't require a meeting. And, the majority of pivotal decisions, are not decided upon, following some enlightening PowerPoint presentation, nor some revelation brought forth after deep discussion (with dozens of employees) around a large circular oak table. Instead, as most of us in the corporate world already know, big decisions and novel, innovative ideas, often surface during secluded self-reflection. Real plans are often rapidly scribbled out on restaurant napkins or arrived at on bar stools. Most interoffice communication occurs via good (old-fashioned) email. Recall our favorite joke again: the acronym CEO usually doesn't stand for "Chief Executive Officer." It stands for "Chief Email Officer."

Other than email interactions, most people prefer individual (and informal) "water cooler" style conversations. Just a few moments spent with five staff members, individually, can be more productive, than gathering everyone together for a lengthy meeting.

But, with this in mind, we have to accept that meetings do indeed play a role in corporate life, as well as the human experience. People have (probably) been coming together, and sitting in a circle to discuss important topics, since man first invented fire. There is value in such exchanges (on a psychological level, if not an economic one). At the very least, attending a meeting with your coworkers is akin to asking them about the weather when you pass them in the hall. Nobody who bloviates about the weather is actually very concerned with the current barometric pressure. Rather, these micro-conversations are the "social lubricant" that allow us to co-exist with our fellow meat-eating mammals, and maintain civility.

When your coworker's ask each other about the weather (or last night's basketball game, or the "wife and kids"), what they're really doing is saying, "Our relationship is ok right?" Your positive, friendly response, is taken as an affirmation to this question. These little "social pings" are a necessary attribute of our daily discourse. And, even if meetings at your workplace only succeed in giving everyone a glimpse of the current state of the group dynamic, and the unifying satisfaction of "group solidarity," then, that alone might be valuable enough to warrant some meetings—despite how frivolous the meeting content actually is.

But, psychological incentives aside, let's discuss some tips that might enable you to get more value out of your team's weekly roundtable.

Tip 1: Make sure each person has a reason to be there.

We train corporate staff to employ OKR principles. Consequently, we think that having an "objective reason" to do things, is kind of important.

If you've spent any amount of time in corporate disturbia, then you've probably found yourself walking into board meetings, for reasons which were never entirely clear to you. So don't do that. Meetings are effective when everyone in the room knows exactly why they are there, and what is to be done. The late great Steve Jobs was famous for ruthlessly (and awkwardly) kicking people out of meetings who (he felt) "didn't need to be there."

So, before the meeting starts, type the agenda out, and email it to everyone. This announcement should never be in the form of a 2,000-word outline (that nobody will read), nor a downloadable PowerPoint presentation (that nobody will download). Instead, the announcement of the initial meeting objectives should be in the form of a two or three-sentence message. If it's longer than that, you're probably doing it wrong. If you feel inclined to list exactly who should attend, then do it.

Tip 2: Don't invite too many humans

Work hard to keep your meetings small. Adding more humans to a room can complicate things. With each *social creature* you add to a room, you increase the *social workload* that every other mind in the room must bear. Meetings work best when the only people in attendance, are the actual people that need to receive the information. Larger companies often add seats along the meeting room walls, where the assistants of upper managers sit, observe, take notes, and (sometimes) scoff. Depending on the type of company you work for, this might be unavoidable. But, we discourage this type of personnel layout. Filling a meeting with unneeded staff often incites negative psychological consequences. Just as filling the bleachers with screaming fans at a baseball game, brings out the competitive, aggressive traits of the home team, filling a room with polarized staff, might incite conversations that are more pugnacious than need be.

Tip 3: Use a timer

Recall Parkinson's Law again:

"Work expands so as to fill the time available for its completion."

You can almost always convey as much important information in a half-hour meeting, as you can in a one-hour meeting. If you give people 10 hours to make a decision, then they *will take* 10 hours. If you give them 10 minutes, then they'll do it in 10 minutes. There may be incidents in which a grand revelation only reveals itself at the 9th hour of a meeting. But, as we've all experienced, this is rare, and typically decisions made in the first hour tend to be the ones we ultimately *go along with* anyway. So keep those meetings short. And use an egg timer (prominently placed at the front of the room), so that everyone will know when "time is up."

Tip 4: Whiteboards are ok, but PowerPoint is not

Much has been written about the horrors of PowerPoint. It's one of those inventions that everybody uses but nobody likes. This is not necessarily the fault of PowerPoint. PowerPoint is a data visualization tool, like any other tool. But, by default, most people are just not very good at the art and science of data visualization itself. You've probably patiently sat through a PowerPoint talk, featuring tawdry animations, jarring transition effects, and (the worst of the worst) slide sound effects. When PowerPoint is bad, it's bad. But, if you get a chance, take a moment to Google the names David McCandless or Hans Rosling. These two men actually know how to do Data Visualization. And for them, the animation enhances the presentation, rather than bore the audience. So don't be too hard on poor old PowerPoint. Instead, simply recognize that most corporate meetings don't warrant the considerable time and skill required to compile a presentation that features slideshow content. Thus, as a rule of thumb, it's almost always better to stick to using the meeting room whiteboard, over any other given piece of technology.

Tip 5: Avoid iPhones and Laptops

My entire life resides in my laptop. Every document and email I've created since 1996, lives in my trusty MSI laptop. I couldn't live without it. I have similar feelings about my iPhone, (unfortunately).

However, laptops and smartphones tend to be too distracting in corporate meetings. Even when notetaking is warranted, the clatter of keyboard keys, and the swiping of screens, often intrudes on an otherwise fluid informational conveyance.

So try this instead: Before the meeting starts, place a brick of plain white printer paper, and several cups of pens and pencils, in the middle of the table. Your goal is to encourage the participants to jot down simple notes and reminders to themselves, on pieces of paper that they can take with them—back to their desk.

To curtail your staff's temptation to obsessively check their phones for text messages and emails, our favorite trick involves placing a sound-proof box near the boardroom door. Each occupant is asked to drop their phone off in the box, until the meeting is over. The sound-proofing is important here, because those phones will "bleep and blop," throughout the meeting. And if your employees can hear the sound, they'll be instantly distracted.

We admit all this appears a bit childish at first. But in this brave new world of never-ending technological dopaminergic distractions, drastic times call for drastic measures.

Tip 6: Try to avoid conference calls

Improvements in broadband internet, phone speakers, and microphone technology, have made conference calls commonplace in the modern office. It's become typical to sit in on a call with ten people (all of whom may work in the same building), and each refusing to leave their cubicle—instead, using the time to play solitaire, while they (half-heartedly) listen to the drone of a plastic headset.

Obviously, something is lost when we use such technology. Sitting across from a plastic speaker will never have the same psychological effect, as sitting across from a human face. Given the international considerations of the modern office, such calls might be unavoidable in your workplace. But, whenever possible, try to avoid such calls.

If time or proximity is an issue, work hard to schedule real face time anyway, or at least, try to minimize the number of people who rely on this manner of communication, in your company. Granted, mankind will probably succeed in eliminating the need for face-to-face interaction someday (and in some industries, he already has). But we're not quite there yet.

Tip 7: End your meeting with written action steps

You may have heard of the infamous 1964 Murder of Kitty Genovese, and the social psychological phenomenon that resulted from it known as "The Bystander Effect." Some say this phenomenon contributed to the death of Kitty, who reportedly pled with her neighbors for help, but was ignored and left to die in a building hallway.

The Bystander Effect happens when a crowd of people all witness the same event, but nobody takes any action—because each person assumes that the other person is "going to do something."

How about another story?

In 1973, John Dean was asked to testify to the Senate Watergate Committee, about any wrongdoings he observed in the Nixon administration. John Dean recalled his interactions with Richard Nixon in vivid detail, and gave a play-by-play rendition of his Oval Office conversations. But later, it was revealed that Nixon had secretly recorded all of his Oval Office meetings. After this revelation, Harvard memory researcher Ulric Neisser compared Dean's testimony to the actual contents of Nixon's tapes. And what he found, became the case study for his book on the failures of human memory. In short, the confidence you may have, about how well your memory works, or how good your recall is of past events, does not coincide with what actually happened in the past. Our memories are colored by the emotions, biases, and prejudices we bring to every interaction. Additionally, each time we lean back and access one of our memories, we change it (just a little bit). And when you execute this "memory retrieval task" (for years and years), then you slowly accumulate a plethora of neuronal alterations—which prevent you from ever truly accurately recalling what *really* happened.

So, what can we learn from these two anecdotes? What does the Murder of Kitty Genovese, and the Watergate testimony of John Dean have to teach us about human interaction? Unfortunately, corporate meetings are susceptible to both of these human flaws.

Have you ever watched a team of employees walk away from a corporate meeting, only to return next week with absolutely nothing done. Why? Because everybody thought the other guy was going to do it.

Have you ever watched two employees in a meeting, arguing about what was discussed in the meeting last week? Have you noticed that each employee is convinced that *his rendition* of the previous meeting is the objectively correct depiction?

Everyone in the corporate world has witnessed such events. They are part and parcel of being a limited human, wrought with quirks of the mind, and failures of memory.

So how can we fix this?

As we discussed earlier, we often prefer to limit the use of technology in most meetings. But we make sure that a vast array of colored pens, and reams of plain white paper adorn the tables of our meeting rooms. So, when it's time to wrap up your meeting, make sure that action steps are assigned to individual employees, or DRIs (Directly Responsible Individuals) as we've disused in previous chapters.

Keep it simple. Grab a piece of paper and write one sentence on it, made up of three bits of information:

1. The name of the DRI (Directly Responsible Individual)
2. The name of the task.
3. And, the date of completion.

For example, the sentence might look like this:

- Jason will "**design our convention flier**" by "**Tuesday**."
- Alexander will "**sign the Dunder Mifflin contract**" by "**next week**."
- Sarah will "**hire a new graphic designer**" by "**February**."

Note how short and simple each action step is. Again, each one contains just three items. The employee's name, the task, and the date of completion.

At the end of each meeting, you should have three or four of such notes. I.e. three or four "actions step sentences" should have been scribed.

To keep things organized, consider pinning each piece of paper onto a corkboard in the meeting room. So, everyone can see what everyone else is working on, and (next week) when you meet again, *nobody* feels obliged to exclaim, "I wasn't responsible for getting that done!"

- By assigning tasks to individual team members (and not to the team), we eliminate the Bystander Effect.
- And, by writing these assignments down on paper, we eliminate the need to rely on errant human memory.

Indeed, even if a task is to be accomplished by several people, it's *still* usually best to just chose one person to be your responsible (DRI).

Once you have pinned each task to your corkboard, don't be afraid to add notes to the page, or alter the goals over time. In the next meeting, if the task has been accomplished, and the paper is no longer useful, then simply throw it away, and move on to new tasks.

Often, you will find that tasks (created in this fashion) will grow and change over time.

- Sometimes a task will spawn a completely new task—the necessity of which was not apparent when the initial task was created.

- Sometimes an employee will get sick, or quit, or be burdened with other pressing issues. In such cases, his name can simply be crossed out. And a new employee name can be written in his place.

- Sometimes a task is so fruitful, that its completion calls for the creation of a whole new department, or opens up a new source of income for your company.

You may feel inclined to alter our above-described system, to better meet the needs of your own organization. Readers with a more technical background might already be using similar task-management systems, like "Scrum." But, whichever system you choose, just make sure that you have *some way* to track and record the objectives, that are decided upon in each meeting.

Ch. 12: Conclusion

Does anything in your life really change, after you watch a rousing movie, or read an inspiring book?

Well… no…

Usually nothing changes.

You have to actually *make use of* the new information, and convert it into something practical and tangible. Merely reading a book will not make you more confident, improve your posture, nor will it help you manage your business. Unless you rigorously work to apply these concepts, your brain's neurons will gradually (and naturally) relinquish all this information, in a matter of weeks.

Humorously, many people think that merely holding the information (in book form) is enough. It has been estimated that only 20% of books that are purchased, are actually ever read. So if you've made it to this point, then, congratulates! Only 1 out of 5 people have come as far as you have. (You must be a wise person indeed!)

Time to Take Action

There are few shortcuts on the road to success. If you want to bring about positive change in your workplace, then only *focused daily action* can help in applying all this new information.

You'll never know if any given technique works for your organization, unless you try it. Not every method will work for every reader. But it is only via "taking action" that you'll know for sure. It is this first step "getting started" that is always the most difficult one. As Mark Twain said:

"The secret of getting ahead is getting started."

In any pursuit, it's on the first couple steps where the vast majority of people stumble. Failure can be scary. But if you hesitate, and miss your opportunity, then you'll never know what could have been.

Avoid Overthinking

So don't spend too much time in contemplation over inconsequential events. Doing more research, and continuously absorbing an infinite sea of information, can (at times) create a false sense of accomplishment.

In a 1929 interview with "The Saturday Evening Post," Albert Einstein said:

"Reading after a certain age diverts the mind too much from its creative pursuits. Any man who reads too much and uses his own brain too little falls into lazy habits of thinking, just as the man who spends too much time in the theater is tempted to be content with living vicariously, instead of living his own life."

It's tempting to fall into this trap.

All the reading and research you've done, will not be of any use to you, if you don't take that first step towards doing something productive. Only enacting a plan of action leads to potential success. As Einstein hinted at, continuing to gather data, without action, is just mere mental laziness and procrastination.

Avoid Procrastination

Procrastination is the act of intentionally putting something off until a later date, even though it should be done right away. Procrastination can derail you from achieving your goals. It can creep up on you without any warning, and it will disguise itself as something else to trick you. For managers, procrastination often comes in the form of "busy work." That is, non-essential work that we insist on doing, while we're avoiding getting the "deep work" done.

On Perfectionism

Perfectionism is another elusive demon you'll meet on your management path. It's also the toughest "management nut" to crack. Because careful consideration of minute details, sometimes does (indeed) increase the value of a product. So there is room in this world for perfectionists. However, the majority of little organizational tweaks (to any given product or team), typically have absolutely no effect on the bottom line. So be cognizant of this phenomenon, and always err on the side of action, rather than pedantic perfectionism.

Be wary of management gimmicks (especially digital ones)

You'll notice, in this book, we have not mentioned any specific management software package, nor have we advised you to invest in any digital devices at all.

This was intentional.

But, the exclusion of software from this book is *not* to imply that we are necessarily against the use of technology in management. Good OKR, SCRUM, SMART, and other corporate task-tracking software does indeed exist. (As well as a flurry of time-management devices, smartphone apps, and various cloud-based employee management systems.)

But, in our experience, the majority of smaller offices could adequately accomplish most management tasks with just a pencil, paper, and a large wall-mounted corkboard.

If your company is growing rapidly, and the *number of employees* is moving into the triple digits, then buying (or developing) in-house management software might be productive. But just be warned, that, if you are not currently successfully tracking your employees with pencil and paper, then digitizing this information is probably not going to help.

So work hard to perfect this process, using "low-tech technology" first. And then consider using the high-tech stuff in the future. Migrating to high-tech solutions is much easier after you already have a firm understanding of the more low-tech goal-setting *modus operandi.*

Take time out for yourself

Finally, as we've already stressed in this book, it's important to take a moment to celebrate the little victories of your employees. But, managers are people too. So, it's also important to celebrate your own victories. As David Deida wrote:

"Every moment of your life is either a
test or a celebration."

Fostering a sense of accomplishment during good times, will help you to keep going during the bad times. Indeed, even micro-victories, like crossing out rows from your to-do list, are moments to allow the *sense of accomplishment* to permeate your consciousness, and reinforce your confidence as a manager.

Outro

Now, we have arrived at the end of this book.

I hope I've been able to impress upon you the immense value that OKRs have to offer. We've attempted to communicate how conventional (non-structured) goal-setting, is usually a detriment to a company, and remains too ambiguous to be productive in a modern office.

But with OKRs, you can create order from this ambiguity, while developing an insanely effective team that is open, accountable, inspired, and motivated to succeed.

By establishing a solid framework for goal-setting, your team will have the necessary guidance to tackle the most challenging tasks, and achieve your most ambitious organizational objectives.

When implemented correctly, OKRs are a powerful business tool—that excel in their ability to encourage both employees *and* managers, to work in harmony, toward a unified corporate vision.

Now you are equipped with the knowledge you need to get going with OKRs, and start building your "dream team."

I wish you luck and great success on your journey.

CPSIA information can be obtained
at www.ICGtesting.com
Printed in the USA
BVHW031119230223
659071BV00009B/577